The Parable of His-Story

The Parable of His-Story

Nick Taylor

BOOKS

Winchester, UK
Washington, USA

First published by O-Books, 2011
O-Books is an imprint of John Hunt Publishing Ltd., Laurel House, Station Approach,
Alresford, Hants, SO24 9JH, UK
office1@o-books.net
www.o-books.com

For distributor details and how to order please visit the 'Ordering' section on our website.

ISBN: 978 1 84694 825 1

A CIP catalogue record for this book is available from the British Library.

Design: Stuart Davies

Printed in the UK by CPI Antony Rowe
Printed in the USA by Offset Paperback Mfrs, Inc

CONTENTS

For all who have gone
before, for all yet to come
and of course, my mum

Beginning at the End

Hello. This is the first in a series of lines that forms a book. It is something I started writing a decade ago but you know how it goes: think about it, have a cup of tea, write a lot of nonsense, cry, laugh, think about it, have a cup of tea.

Now it's July and the sun is out. I'm sitting outside a café in Brighton. The headline of the local paper reads 'Driver Blames Crash on Bee'. A picture of Mrs. Thatcher in the style of the Sex Pistols adorns a cushion. It's one of those ordinary summer days by the sea. Five gulls glide above me. A couple on the next table order orange juice. All seems well with the world.

Only it isn't. Children are being stabbed and killing themselves and being swept away by tsunamis, tornados and ongoing war. Ordinary climatic shift is propelled to cataclysmic levels by the worldwide need to go faster. The economy is flat-lining and the idea of borrowing to jump-start it is redundant because borrowing is all we've been doing. Food prices are escalating, seas are drying up, icecaps are melting, and the bees, when they're not being accused of causing road accidents, are disappearing. People are exhausted. Fear is endemic. The tap water tastes of bleach.

This information isn't new and for some people is already inspiring them to make changes at the personal level: sourcing renewable energy, growing vegetables, living more lightly with the land. For many of us, even the humble trip to the bathroom is accompanied by a new consciousness to switch the tap off as we brush. We're good, see; look at how quick we pick it up! But to go beyond swapping a few light bulbs and only partially filling the kettle seems an enormous, expensive nuisance; another burden added to the stress of commuting, computing and juggling childcare.

In the circles of addiction recovery programs much is made of the psychological state of denial. One of the favored analogies is the elephant filling the room that no one talks about. It's what psychologist Eviatar Zerubavel calls a 'conspiracy of silence ... whereby a group of people tacitly agree to outwardly ignore something of which they are all personally aware'. But becoming conscious is to risk seeing what's staring all of us in the face. The stark situation facing individuals, societies and the whole planet is that something very big and very old is coming to an end. What this 'something' is forms the title of this book. How it affects every one of us is the choice we are being asked to make.

The point of this work is threefold. Firstly, it is to show the limited story that has shaped the environment and attitudes we take as everlasting. Stories have power. They have the ability to influence minds and give body to ways of being. They make our world just as an architect's scribble can build a city. One particular story has dominated a historically datable period of around 5,000 years. We think of this last age as history, and indeed it is. It's his-story, the period of time where men have been in charge. This story of his includes Judaism, Christianity, Islam, materialism, communism and capitalism, and all the repeated and disputed theories of each. But it is all one story: the story of the dominance of the masculine, frightened to the point of war with what it sees as its opposite. The key attributes of the masculine age took root around 5,000 years ago and shaped the world by using the following tools: the written word, agriculture, cities, private property, war, hereditary monarchy and a monotheistic (belief in one god) worldview. So successful has the masculine mindset been that many of us consider these tools eternal and see no way for life to function without them. The physical promotion of his-story, through self-justifying reason, financial power and violent strife, has led us to see this way of life and its implications as staying with us forever.

The second purpose of this tale is to move from the dusty catacombs of Ancient Mesopotamia (where it all started) and sweep us through thousands of years of his-story in action up to the present. It will show how the same stories that began to be told all those millennia ago are being repeated today. Whether in terms of our diet, anxieties around our bodies, attitudes to animals, children and Nature in general, our sense of gender and sexuality, his-story is a current force negatively affecting each of us. A story that elevates the masculine while forbidding, alienating and negating the feminine is fatally unbalanced. 2011 AD is not 2011 BC but the parallels between then and now are striking. The lion's share of the wealth in the hands of a few men; frequent war between neighboring states over rival ideologies; an irrational but pervading sense that women are less than men; abuse of animals and Nature to secure the power base of the successful few... his-story is as current today as at any point over this last age. At a time when the planet herself is gently, but firmly, asking us to change our patterns of thought and behavior, the continuation of the telling of his-story threatens the sustained existence of all life on Earth.

But this is a threefold tale. It would be cold comfort to be told the root and symptoms of the problem without being offered some sort of remedy. The third point to this book is to suggest possible solutions to the various separate but related crises we face as a planet. His-story has now pervaded every continent, every family and every idea and brought us to this lip of annihilation. Yet it is in the telling of this story that the seed of renewal lies. If the last age has told us one story, unbalanced and aggressive, then the time is approaching for other stories to be remembered. Prehistory might be a vague, ill-documented terrain, but it stays with us; in the land and in our dreams, in those persistent, least-explored memories, and in the whispers of thousands of distant tribes. To bring the feminine back into balance is to pay attention to the stories of indigenous cultures, to listen to the more subtle voices and to re-imagine the possibilities that exist. It is not to replace his-story with her-story. It is not to use the language of the former to hammer out a parody of the alternative. If his-story has fought to create a one-world, globalized, hegemonic state, the possible alternatives are necessarily plural. The remedies to the dogmatic repetition of his-story are tales from each of us, willing to promote tolerance and equality, valuing all life as we wish ourselves to be valued, seeing the world as a gift, not a soulless resource to be run into the ground. To encourage the resurgence of the feminine is about welcoming the circle as well as the straight line, to embrace the infinite spiral as well as the male need to order beginnings and endings, to open our lives up to dance and play, and to remember how to respect the life force in every creature, plant and element.

What is being asked of us is nothing less than to rewire our conscious circuitry and remember other ways of living with the world. What is needed most is the humility to accept that we might have got it terribly wrong. What is at stake is the survival of all life on Earth.

Despite the terror that his-story has inspired, and despite the fury one is likely to feel at the long succession of this imbalance, our well-being rests on forgiving this limited experiment in unfettered masculinity. If we are to learn from it, we need to understand where we've been and what's brought us to this point of near extinction, and we need to safely express our anger, grief and remorse at the atrocities committed. But if we are to move on we need to forgive, to recognize that we all make mistakes and that alongside all the brilliant and bonkers attributes of being human comes an unfailing capacity to err.

The remedies to move away from self-destruction rest with every one of us. It is everyone's responsibility to make the next step, to use the wonderful creative power of our humanity to remember how else we may live well with the world.

It's fitting that this takes the form of the written word, a form that, from ancient law codes and holy guidebooks to free daily newspapers, has defined this age. But these words are written with a desire not to browbeat or berate us into frigid impotence, but to empower any person who reads them. We need more than ever to let go of what no longer serves us, embrace what is elemental to our survival, and dare to discover the difference. In short, we need to begin again.

It's a big claim. It is not made lightly. Five thousand years is a massive sweep, and the ten summers since I started writing this are as long as *Big Brother* has existed. These ten years have offered several chances to put pen to paper and, each time, ordinary human doubt and my own gift for error have kept them hidden. Now, however, is the time.

I have a common name and am frequently mistaken for a mythic band member from the 1980s pop group Duran Duran. I was born in Wales, read Modern History at Oxford, and have since grown to weave a spiritual practice into my daily life. But who I am is less important than what is being said. I could be any of us. I'm the person who juggles a take-away coffee as they remember to call their mum, the one engrossed with their iPhone and struggling with a rucksack full of too much stuff. I am the voice that finds its way to your tongue when you didn't expect it. I am the sound of a distant memory you never knew you had singing in your blood. The UK birthed and grew me, and it is her language and landscape I know by heart. But as his-story has spread across the world, so the lessons from this age find echoes in every island and continent across the globe. More than a cheap political soundbite and more than ever before, we are, as a whole planet, in this together.

A number of other writers, thinkers and storytellers are quoted here. They might not all be happy about this and so I am faced with a fittingly paradoxical task. If people are unhappy with my interpretations of their words then all responsibility begins and ends with me. Any mistakes and misinterpretations are mine alone. But if people agree with what is said then I bow in gratitude to their skills as my teachers. These ideas were loaned to me from them. I was able to make this journey joining up the dots from across this age on the stones they laid before me.

I don't know how long this will take to type nor how long to read. Maybe now's the time to put the kettle on. This is where it begins ...

Apples and Pairs

It's odd to think of a time that wasn't dominated by plasma screens, but come with me now. Let's watch cars and roads disappear. Oops, there goes the gun. We're moving back, watching mosaics return to unbaked mud, aqueducts unarch themselves. Metal is back in the ground, houses are rare and where they do appear are circular and made simply of wood and straw. Strange beasts have reappeared, the stars are abundant, trees and plants are lush and everywhere. We are back at the beginning.

Rather, we are back at where for thousands of years we have understood and been taught it all began.

In the beginning was the word. It's a pleasing place for a book to start. It sets the scene. And here we are. Genesis: the first book of the Old Testament in *The Bible*. So long taken as gospel truth that to disagree with it was to face your soul's damnation, and to swear honesty involved putting your hand on it. What does it tell us about how this age of men began?

It tells us there was a supreme being, one God, whose first action was to split the world up, separating light from dark and water from land. It was this male god who made the animals, fashioned a man out of clay (Adam) and, taking a rib from his body, made a companion for him (Eve). There they are: the first couple, the David and Victoria Beckham of early history, naked and unashamed in paradise. Now it doesn't matter whether you believe this story anymore or not. What matters is that for thousands of years people did. The power of a thing rests in the belief it is imbued with. Nor is this about entering the contemporary fray of science versus religion. It's about being able to map where we are by tracing a finger along the route by which we've come.

God instructed man to have dominion over the rest of life,

saying, 'Be fruitful and increase, fill the earth and subdue it, rule over the fish in the sea, the birds of heaven and every living thing that moves across the earth.' The single male god allowed Adam and Eve to eat all of it, apart from the fruit of the Tree of the Knowledge of Good and Evil. But Eve was tempted by the serpent (Satan, in his earliest role), took a bite of the apple, offered it to Adam who also took a bite and BAM! God's wrath! Expulsion from paradise! The Fall! The world is ruined and it appears to be the woman's fault. When Adam and Eve left paradise it was with a fig leaf and a pressing burden of guilt. This was the original sin, and generations of people have carried this shame. Disasters, violence, war, barbarity, misconception, parking tickets – all accompanied by the nagging voice of the single male god saying, 'You are guilty!'

So Eve was the first woman and made from Adam's spare rib. Not only do we find the supreme being of this story a male god, but woman is an afterthought who has to bear direct responsibility for everything bad in the world. Her complicity with Satan implies she is at best weak and at worst evil. The story of our beginnings that has dominated the western world made a villain of the female and the feminine against the *good* god. Suddenly the guilt weighs heavier on women, and successive generations of men are instructed to beware them – those snakes in the grass – as well as the femininity within their own bodies. The feminine quality of life, every mother who gives birth, Mother Nature herself, is damned by this tale as the cause of all things bad.

The idea that the biblical spin on our beginnings involves a male god playing with clay means we lose a feeling of connection with the Earth that raises and supports us, and means Adam went without a belly button. It is a first base that has been effortlessly assimilated into the western worldview for thousands of years. What begins with this story of our origins is power: the potential to decide and determine what will come to pass and to define the essential nature of what will be. With Mother Earth nowhere present in the beginning of our creation story, with Eve damned as evil, and with Adam first out into the world and ready to explain his origins without recourse to woman, the definitions from the word go were in the mouths of men.

Let's look again at the trees in the Garden of Eden. Aren't they pretty! Oh look, there are two of them: the fabled Tree of the Knowledge of Good and Evil and the Tree of Life. Why these two trees? Why the difference and why these abstract concepts? *Good* and *evil* are sewn into the fabric of our understanding of the world by this first story like nametapes in PE kits. We've grown so used to these words, restated through the changing millennia and handily dispatched to cover everything from a new religion to a style of dress, that we would be forgiven for not giving much thought to what they mean, whether they make sense and, more pressingly to us at this time of transition, whether or not they are useful anymore. Good and evil, one of the pairs that ripple out from the beginning of the world to join the myriad other pairings: man/woman, God/Satan, light/dark, heaven/hell and right/left. God might be in the singular but everywhere else the narrative splits: up/down, out/in, sun/moon and so on. What is interesting is not that we live in a world of opposites but that the most dominant and enduring written code about them should afford them an associated morality and set them against each other to slog it out.

The potency of (literally) eating the fruit of the knowledge of good and evil has been one of the most powerful but least questioned aspects of this last age. It bequeathed to us a value judgment on the poles that balance the world. It encouraged us to run towards one and away from the other in a way that, were the world a ship, would cause the vessel to list before capsizing. To elevate one side (the masculine, good god, with its associations of reason and light) against the other (feminine, the devil, bad, mysterious and dark) not only divided the world: it set the whole at war with itself. If the eating of such fruit precipitated

The Fall, then the continued consumption of good and evil is the diet we've used to poison the world and all its life forms.

It's a sunny day today. I like the sun. I like the shade too. If everything has suffered this sunder, which is good: sun or shade? Which am I allowed to be, warm or cool? Which is preferable, light or dark? Only when we examine the duality present everywhere under the Tree of the Knowledge of Good and Evil does the tree itself begin to look problematic. The process of the other tree, Life, renders morality at best temporary and relative. If you're baking hot, to be in the shade is great. And if you're shivering cold, to be out in the warmth of the sun is an equal relief. Both poles are necessary and, depending on the situation, both can be embraced with gratitude.

The absolute certainty of good and evil has been wonderfully tricked recently by black culture, whose own heritage on the moral scale, as we will later see, was once decreed by the ruling whites as *savage* and for whom different skin color was enough to justify their mass enslavement. The word *wicked* has been inverted. What was once used as a synonym for *evil* became used to describe its opposite. *Bad, sick, ill, bare* – these words are all making similar leaps to the other pole of meaning. Not only is morality revealed as a slippery concept; the very words summoned to solidify it slip away before our mouths.

Maybe it's time to give more attention to the Tree of Life. A much simpler-sounding tree: no prohibitions here. Life in its natural state has no concept of shame or guilt. There is no moral code attached to the behavior of a bee or an acorn. Life is in leaf, wing and scale perfect, evolving, procreative and mortal. Life has grass, coral and snake, and all of them do their do (waving, growing, winding), without being chased off the island with sticks. Whereas the Tree of the Knowledge of Good and Evil set in to tax us, the Tree of Life was not mentioned again. Where did it go? What exactly has been going on for all these thousands of years and why does this matter to where we find ourselves today?

Of course, many people think the Bible is quaint but no more a work of fact than *Footballer's Wives.* If we're going to explore how this age began we might need to do some serious digging.

Ur …

The natural world, women and the feminine have long suffered from the excessive imbalance of a story that told of its male god and man as all things good. How long this story has been dominant depends on when and where in the world it took hold. But to go back to its inception is to take a journey back to the Middle East, back around 5,000 years to the 'cradle of civilization'.

Ancient Mesopotamia is an interesting place to visit. The city of Ur is one of the earliest cities of this age and isn't far from contemporary headlines, now better known as Basra in Iraq. Five thousand years ago several apparently disparate but related events converged to mark the beginning of his-story. Studies of surviving writing and remains show that around 3000 BC a new way of being in the world was taking hold: one that favored men and the masculine at the direct expense of women and the feminine.

Why the following ingredients came together at the same time is open to speculation. Was this a cosmic movement, a shift akin to moving from one season to another, much like the shift happening to us now? Did one development come before the others or did they rise at once? What is apparent is that once these changes took place they became self-supporting and immensely attractive to many would-be male leaders all over the world.

Much like the separation that marks the opening lines of Genesis, division was one of the first ideas of this new age. Land was separated from sea, and that land began to be seen as capable of further separation. There was land that could be farmed as opposed to land that was wilderness. Fencing off the land enabled crops and animals to be seen as private property, encouraging the division between his corn and theirs. While the concept of agriculture is widely considered to have come after the end of the last ice age (around 10,000 years ago when the climate warmed), many people look to the date of 5,000 years ago because that's when another invention took root which provided historically verifiable records: the invention of cuneiform writing (pictograms that became increasingly abstract until they looked like the alphabet we know and use today).

It could well be that the movement to own land and property provided an impetus for the men doing the carving-up to keep a better record of their new wealth. Certainly private ownership brought other factors into play. With division sprung up competition and hierarchy. With property came fear of its loss and the need for armed gangs to protect the wealth. Another development from around 5,000 years ago is a further signifier of this last age: the rise of armed forces, violent struggle and warfare.

With fear around the loss of the new wealth, men needed to take charge of their land more definitely, giving rise to deforestation and the erecting of buildings in stone and wood. City building also developed around this point, gathering people together in fixed areas and prompting the emergence of powerful temple-palace elites who controlled grain, gold and the information about them. Not everyone was happy with these new developments, least of all the women and the Goddess-following pagan tribes of the previous age. The temple-palace elites set about justifying the changes, enshrining them with their new words into law codes and books of religion. The new elites needed a mandate for the overthrow of the old ways and developed the model of a single male god to echo the single male warrior-king who was rapidly using his new wealth to enshrine himself as lord over all.

The new technique of writing was quickly put to use by covering tablets of stone with new rules and edicts, limiting the power of women and forbidding those actions which supported pagan habits and polytheism (belief in many gods). All those who collaborated with the new changes would be rewarded and those who threatened them would be punished. The most powerful man in the new system elevated other men to positions near him to ensure he had practical support to keep his land, his throne and his riches. Matrilineal descent was removed and patriarchy triumphed. The riches of the father were now to be inherited by the son. The final limiter to man's new limitless ambition, death, was cheated by a system of male-centered hereditary inheritance.

Why should any of these things matter now? Firstly, because for many people in the 21st century the idea of living without cities, the written word, agriculture, armies, social structure and a male-god-centered religion seems absurd if not impossible. There is still a powerful narrative to what went on before his-story that depicts people with matted beards grunting in caves, fending off angry animals and being generally miserable. It makes us feel less empowered about changing our lives if we imagine the alternative to be so gruesome. Another reason why these developments need to be investigated is the uncanny sense of connection between them. What they challenged was a way of living in the world that was established: a plethora of local tribes, guided by Goddesses as well as Gods, living in harmony with the rest of Nature. What they brought about was the means to rule the world by men. The creation of patriarchy established rule over the many and multiform by the select and the same, and ushered in a singular idea of what it meant to be a man. Finally, as this age has succeeded in bringing about many so-called 'advancements', including poverty, war and ecological devastation, maybe we stand the best chance of moving on from it by understanding its components.

There was a long tradition, pre-history, of songs, poems and stories. The oral tradition isn't useful for historians, nor lawyers, because it isn't written, but it's the way people communicate with each other. Words and sounds flow together in ways that are parochial and variable, sometimes sensible and sometimes fantastic. Not so the written word.

What cuneiform writing did was evolve a means of depiction that increasingly became abstracted from Nature. Images now resembled letters, which could then be reconfigured to make words for abstract concepts (such as *good* and *evil*) that needed no root in the natural world. So the tendency to separate the world in judgment, as well as for ownership and profit, and the tendency to develop a system of written language to record it, went hand in hand. Nor was cuneiform writing as poetic and free as oral language. If something was written on a tablet of stone, it gained weight. It could be held up as an example, used to bind people to the law of its letters, and only those men who were on side with the new tool of thinking could carve the shapes and decipher their meanings.

Surgeon and storyteller Leonard Shlain sees the connection between writing and the rise of a single male god religion. In his book *The Alphabet versus the Goddess*, he suggests that cuneiform writing fosters a patriarchal outlook. All the tools needed to understand, write and read cuneiform writing are in the masculine side of the brain. In developing a system of writing that promoted the masculine side, culture became masculinized. In terms of our own lexicography, the association of the word *right* to mean both *right-hand side* and *correct* is a powerful example of how imbalance was literally written into the word. In Italian, *sinistra* means *sinister* as well as *left*, while in French *gauche* means *left* and also *clumsy*. Even up to the middle of the 20th century, many people were made to change the hand they wrote with, warned that the left hand was the devil's hand. Writing was not the simple arrival of a new tool to aid human society. In developing cuneiform writing, the masculine tool acclaimed its own *right* by denigrating its feminine partner.

Cities, architecture and temple building were also part of this growth of the masculine. The more that the natural world was seen as being under man's dominion, the more man needed places to gather, hoard and rule the product of his property. Writing recovered from Ancient Sumer indicates that increasingly land was controlled by temple-palace households. Those with the most land would secure the strongest power base and ensure they had grain and gold to pay for armed bands of men and keep themselves lords of all. As historian Gerda Lerner notes in *The Creation of Patriarchy*:

> From 3000 BC on, temple hierarchies coordinated the construction and maintenance of a system of canals that were many miles long and demanded the co-operation of a number of communities. The financing of such vast enterprises, the maintenance of labor squads paid in rations and the investment of surpluses in the mass production of certain craft products for export, all led to the consolidation of power and the specialization of function in the hands of a temple bureaucracy.

Though the land had the resources, man's clever use of it demanded organization. There was undoubtedly money to be made. Thousands of years later, specialization would become one of the watch words of Adam Smith's book *The Wealth of Nations*, showing how we are capable of increased productivity when limited to being repeating cogs in a vast machine. But specialization also increases boredom, a sense of depersonalization and loss of power. Cities, like vast irrigation systems, were the most obvious development to ensure stability, control and conspicuous demonstration of material wealth. Much of contemporary urban living owes its reality to these pioneers 5,000 years ago. It's also worth remembering at this time of ecological crisis that, hand in hand with booming cities, the vanishing of bodies of water like the entire Aral Sea is a result of irrigation systems.

It wasn't just in Mesopotamia that these changes took place. In

China a similar development happened around 2500 BC. The Yellow Emperor honored the Three August Ones, whose gifts were central to the power of the Xia, Shang and Zhou dynasties. Fu Xi was responsible for animal husbandry, marriage and administration; Shannong for agriculture and medicine; and Yu for engineering and irrigation. And across the world, whether through charging empires or copying the neighbors, similar developments arose.

The rise of social stratification was another development of the unchecked masculine. Fixed castes were needed to keep people in their ordered places, ensuring that the wealth of the newly powerful father was passed down to the son. As French philosopher Simone de Beauvoir writes in *The Second Sex*, 'From the day agriculture ceased to be an essentially magic operation and first became creative labour, man realised he was a generative force and laid claim to his children and his crops simultaneously.' This idea secured another apparently eternal, though culturally specific, rite: marriage. The new social contract exchanged male loyalty for female chastity. After all, the man who'd begun to carve up the world for his own gain needed to be assured the male child who would inherit was actually his.

The practice of hereditary power that enshrined leadership in the hands of fathers and sons is once more datable to around 5,000 years ago. As chiefs emerged in Mesopotamia and sought to fix their power by emphasizing social hierarchy, so the Indo-Aryans set up this system in India. It is generally agreed that between 3000 BC and 2500 BC the Vedic culture developed in India at the expense of that of the Indus. The Indo-Aryan (Vedic) culture gave rise to the Vedas ('books of wisdom') and a dominant single system, Advaita ('the one truth'). What else we know of the Aryans is that there was continuous fighting between them. They divided their world into different kingdoms and fought among themselves for extensions of their territories and power. It is with the Indo-Aryans that the system of social stratification changed. Prior to this date there are three broad divisions – warriors, priests and commoners – but professions were not hereditary, nor were there restrictions on marrying and dining. With the arrival of the Aryans came class distinctions that froze according to your family of birth. Practically, this meant an end to children finding their own way in the world according to talent and inclination. According to the Vedic philosophy there were now *Brahmins, Kshatriyas, Vaishyas* and *Shudras*. Separation extended beyond profession to whom you could mingle, marry and break bread with. To keep control, the newly masculinized culture needed everyone clearly labeled and staying in their boxes.

The development of solar mythology, forging a link between the king of the land and the king of the sky, ensured a spiritual mandate for a very practical revolution. The association around 5,000 years ago between temple and palace suggest that the wresting of power from the old way happened on both the material and spiritual planes simultaneously. Violent physical control is not to everyone's tastes, which would make it necessary to have a divine presence endorsing the trend. Such a *lord god* would need to be heard and the temple-palaces were where the development of writing took place, which greatly strengthened the leadership role of the elite and made the reality of this new solar god dependent on the written word. News of the *one true god* would come hot off the tablets, with promises of material benefits for those who signed up. To ensure the theology had added muscle, groups of paid thugs were on hand to bully the unbelievers. The most powerful lord needed this most powerful god on his side. So the association between spiritual and material wealth in the hands of a single male began to be accepted. Soon the strongest of the chieftains would set themselves up as king, usurping power over the temples and treating temple property as their own.

Against the new system of private property, written codes,

temple-palace hierarchies and paid men having their violence rewarded with riches, the Great Goddess began to lose power. The earliest written accounts (in the form of *The Epic of Gilgamesh*, for example, approximately 5,000 years ago) prove intimations of her fall. Her consort had, until then, been weak: a son and a lover; discarded and resurrected. Now this male figure rapidly gained size, stature and power until he usurped her. It was now women and the feminine who were weak, no match for the brute physicality of the masculine unchecked by its own balancing agencies of feminine mercy and compassion. The masculine trait of hunting – so focused, unflinching and crucial in the nomadic wilds – turned, in more settled, agricultural environments, to other prey. The Goddess, Mother Earth, and the smaller, humbler and more vulnerable tribes would not withstand the assault.

With the rise of separation came the concept of gender inequality. The masculine was powerful and the feminine was powerless so when he became owner of the land, man claimed also ownership of women. This ownership extended to those of the male sex who were enslaved. The Greek philosopher Aristotle was so confident in the innate division of power that he asserted humanity was always divided into *either* masters *or* slaves. As Lerner says, 'The lifelong dependency of women on fathers and husbands became so firmly established in law and custom as to be considered "natural" and "god-given".' One of these written legal codes, *The Code of Hammurabi* (1750 BC), reflects a class-based society in which women's status wholly depends on the male family head's social status and property.

Five thousand years ago his-story began. The beginning was a schism, after which man saw himself as separate from the Earth and took control of land, animals, women and other men. He began to write, to tally what he owned and to legislate, to enshrine his control on unarguable tablets of stone. He began to separate the wilderness from the farm, began to gather his forces in cities and began to build temples to the mirror of his power: his sole, solar god. He began to marshal his troops and he began to expand. In Mesopotamia, by the time of the Akkadian period (2334–2160 BC) small city-states had given way to large centralized kingdoms that held control over extensive trading networks and vast expanses of territory. The king Naram-Sin needed another title to proclaim for himself and the successfully masculinized empire over which he ruled. He took the normal titles of kingship, including the lofty title *King of the Universe*. But unlike his predecessors Naram-Sin also took an even grander title: *god*. The male hierarchy had established itself and the only being greater than man was the single male divinity who would come to dominate this age.

And the rest, as we shall see, is his-story …

Monotheism for Beginners

The belief in a single male deity has been central to the development of this age. It rose, embryonic, out of Mesopotamia and became formalized over the course of the ensuing millennia. In *The Epic of Gilgamesh* the male hero is on his way to god-like status, defeating the Nature god Humbaba by making the first strike against the cedar tree in his forest. He wins the support of the goddess Ishtar, who pledges herself and her power to him, saying, 'Kings, rulers and princes will bow down before you.' Gilgamesh's ally is Shamash, a solar deity, and his slaying of the monster a motif of male triumph over the feminine dragon. The tree is cut down, the monster is killed and the masculine hero triumphs.

But it is in *The Bible* that the narrative of one god is centralized as traditional oral myths are retold with the omnipotent deity having a starring role. In the story of Abraham (from around 2000 BC), the covenant between Yahweh (the Jewish god) and his people is revealed. The power of this new faith is demonstrated in the book of Deuteronomy. As theological historian Karen Armstrong describes it in *The History of God*, 'If they obeyed Yahweh's laws, he would bless them and bring them prosperity but if they deserted him the consequences would be devastating.' This idea of trading with a single divinity must have had great appeal to a people beset with a changing climate of new warlords with powerful armies. They quickly chose a side and all the images, idols and fertility symbols of goddess cults were removed from the temples and hurriedly burned.

Bucking the tradition of fertility goddesses to help women conceive, it is the male god who now has the power to allow Abraham's wife Sarah to give birth. And with the staying of Abraham's hand, as he is about to sacrifice his son Isaac, so Yahweh intervenes to honor his promise that Abraham will father a nation, on the condition that his male people sacrifice their foreskin. The ancient tradition of selective human sacrifice is usurped by Yahweh and replaced by genital mutilation for all. As Lerner says, 'The image of the breasts of the fertility goddess nurturing the earth and the fields has been replaced by the image of the circumcised penis signifying the covenant contract between mortal man and God.' The male god is born and out go all the links with the mother, the female and the feminine.

Father of psychoanalysis, Sigmund Freud, made connections between Moses, the father of Judaism alongside Abraham, and the radical Egyptian pharaoh Akhenaten, who rebelled against ages of polytheistic belief. Freud picked up the similarity between two apparently separate stories, viewing Moses as an Egyptian who transmitted Akhenaten's religion to the tribes of Israel. Others, like the historian Ahmed Osman, have gone further, implying that Moses was Akhenaten. Either way, the period between 2000 BC and 1000 BC in Egypt is when monotheism began its earliest advance to the detriment of any other form of worship.

Akhenaten overturned the polytheistic belief system of Egypt, which celebrated an assortment of deities and honored gods in animal form. Akhenaten saw the light. Literally. He found the Aten, discovered the world's dependence on light and believed it could be understood as the central principle from which all was derived. But with light he committed himself to the visible and denied everything else: darkness, the afterlife, and the deities of the pantheon like Amun, *the Hidden One*. Akhenaten stood up and proclaimed that the only true god was Aten-Ra, the sun god. He said there was no other god and that he, Akhenaten, was as unique as god because there was no other king as great as him. He changed his name in honor of the deity and began a systematic purge of anyone who thought differently. Akhenaten's remits for his monotheism prefigured a familiar refrain over future crusades, jihads and religious missions. There was no other god but him and no feminine partner. He established a male-dominated cult and systematically attacked other deities or anyone who believed differently. The attacks, which entailed closing temples and dispatching artisans to hack out inscriptions, required the active support of armies. Not for the first or last time, the push towards one male god necessitated military and political coordination.

Whether it was Akhenaten or Moses who led his people out of Egypt, or whether indeed they were one and the same, monotheism was mobile. Moses climbed Mount Sinai where he was given a sign of Yahweh's existence, in the form of a burning bush, and took down the codes for his people, which would become the Ten Commandments. The first two commandments are intrinsic to the nature and legacy of monotheism:

> God spoke, and these were His words:
>
> I am the LORD your God who brought you out of Egypt, out of the land of slavery.
>
> You shall have no other god or gods to set against me.
>
> You shall not make a carved image for yourself nor the likeness of anything in the heavens above, or on the earth below or in the waters under the earth.
>
> You shall not bow down to them or worship them; for I, the LORD your God, am a jealous god. I punish the children for the sins of the fathers.

Every child to whom I've asked the question, 'If you were god, what would your first commandment be?' suggests, 'Don't kill'. But monotheism had other priorities. The commandments quoted above ensured that the widespread Goddess cultures of the time, with their many gods in human and animal form, would be banned and their followers forced to convert or die. The carved image relates to depicting gods in drawn and sculpted form, because while the written word was still a novelty, and not everyone understood a selection of squiggles on a stone, most would recognize the shape of a cat. The earlier development of cuneiform writing was most successfully codified at Mount Sinai. From Sinai onwards this male god proscribed the making of all images. He sanctified only written words. It is not mere coincidence that the first book written in an alphabet is the Old Testament. The moral division between words (*good*) and pictures (*bad*) echoes the division of the world under his-story, where one side is enforced and the other forbidden. Drawing, the making of pictures, a preserve of the left (and feminine) side of the body, was outlawed.

It takes time to establish a new religion, but it helps to win over men if one of the doctrines of it is the suppression of women and the elevation of themselves. The bands of kings looking to legitimize their power knew they could do a lot worse than embrace a doctrine that wrote misogyny into its opening line. As Judaism took hold in the Near East, its main protagonists were men, its central godhead was male and the tool of the masculine brain, the written word, was the means by which he was approached. Yahweh was so powerful that his name could barely be spoken, let alone fully written or, god-forbid, drawn. Slowly, steadily, monotheism became the dominant religion of the Near East. Whereas around 1500 BC there were hundreds of goddess-based sects enveloping the Mediterranean basin, by the 5th century AD they had been almost completely eradicated, by which time women were also prohibited from conducting a single major sacrament.

It isn't that the male or masculine qualities are *bad*, just that honoring only half of the world and running scared from the other creates imbalance. The opposites are harmonized in Nature, a movement most easily enjoyed at the transitional moments of sunrise and sunset. Choose to make it about one rather than both and you destabilize the whole. And if you want to see the consequences of protracted imbalance, switch on a news channel or pick up a paper.

When the pressures of military conflict receded, the old way would resurface. People would gather, feast and dance. They might even carve a picture, the devils. But the determination of the monotheists to enforce the truth as they saw it, and the growing military need to expand and acquire that accompanied it, meant subjugation always returned. Even in Ancient Greece, where polytheism still existed, there were reminders of how the world was changing. The all-powerful god was a father sky god, Zeus: defeater of his own father Cronos and heralded as king of the gods. While Greek culture celebrated the different poles of reason and mystery through Apollo and Dionysus, both gods were male. The elevated philosophy of the Greeks was founded on autochthonic birth – the arrival of a ready-formed state of being, unsullied by relationship with others or the messy business of women. The removal of the mother from the primal scene was an act of symbolic matricide, most commonly seen in the way women were denied full rights of citizenship. What follows in the western philosophical canon, from Plato and Aristotle onwards, is, as the French philosopher Jacques Derrida has it, 'a yarn of suns and sons'.

The ideal city-state in Greece was philosophized as separate and governed homogeneously men for men. The loftiest ideals of democracy were built on the principle of slavery. As the pigs on George Orwell's *Animal Farm* would appreciate, all people were equal but some were more equal than others. This inequality was strengthened by the Roman Empire, whose concepts of martial power, exploitation and violence traced its lineage back to the birth of civilization and prefigured every successive western empire from Christendom to Capitalist American. The rulers were overwhelmingly male and only those men who embodied the most masculine traits held onto power. The established imbalance was codified and enshrined in legislation. The rule of empire, overthrowing indigenous tribes, became an armed sport, where people and land were prizes to enrich the masculinized state. Any pursuits reminiscent of goddess culture were treated with suspicion. Peace was considered weak, tenderness exploited and dancing forbidden. The masculine sun burned strong.

While Jesus arrived to spread the love (encouraging dancing and showing himself merciful), the established Christian church that came to power in Byzantium and Rome married an edited myth of Jesus with a masculine power structure to create a church hierarchy that moved from tolerance to inquisition, from Gnostic self-discovery to dominant orthodoxy. Christianity lost both the loving solidarity and communal ecstasy that enriched its early years. The recognition of Mary as Mother of God was a remembrance of the feminine, like the harmonizing of Christian festivals with pagan ones in Europe to ensure popular approval. Both were compromises that sat increasingly ill with more organized and masculine empires, and once Martin Luther's Reformation took hold in Northern Europe, were corrected. In Catholicism and Protestantism, Mary Magdalene was airbrushed from the story; her role as a close disciple, even partner, to Jesus, doctored (like the translation of her name from 'strengthened with towers' into 'prostitute'). In Dan Brown's novel *The Da Vinci Code,* the revelations that Mary Magdalene is seated to Jesus' right in Leonardo da Vinci's *The Last Supper* and was Jesus' partner, even the mother of his child, might seem fantastic. All too evident are the painted images of Jesus' disciples in caves in Turkey, where those of Mary Magdalene have been violently disfigured. And though all twelve disciples wrote their story of Jesus, only four were considered worthy of inclusion in the gospels. Until the discovery of the Gospel of St. Thomas in 1945 there was little thought given to why two thirds of the disciples had been silenced.

The power of the Christian church under Constantine in the 3rd century AD was codified by pacts sealing physical might with spiritual authority. On Christmas Day in 800 AD, Pope Leo

III crowned the army chief, Charlemagne, Emperor of Christendom. After the Protestant Reformation in England, Mary, the saints and their days, the relics, icons and pictures of Catholic Christianity were ripped down, discredited, sold off and shattered. The reforming church returned worship to the word and enforced a puritan work ethic that suited the expanding, mercantile labor market of colonial Europe. The Reformation renewed a vision of divinity that involved, as Armstrong says, 'a hyperactive awareness of sin and an obsession with Hell ... a frightening God who had predestined all men except the elect to eternal damnation'.

Islam arose around 600 AD to offer a less compromising monotheistic form. There would be no interceding figures, no saints and no feminine iconography. Once Islam felt sufficiently established in 629 AD, a group of men and their leader were dispatched by the Prophet to destroy the statue of the Goddess Fortune in the temple at Mecca. Once more there was the written word in the form of *The Qur'an*, already being marshaled to the interests of a power base and rapidly supplanted with additional and supporting texts (*the Hadith*) to ensure socio-political as well as spiritual control. Indubitable authenticity was written into the beginning of the work. At the start of *the Qur'an* is the crucial sentence: 'This book is not to be 'doubted.' Whatever the inspiration of Mohammed to develop a new religion, quickly the realities became a power struggle between diverging elites, the Sunni and Shia factions arising within a century of the Prophet's death. Judaism, Christianity and Islam all begin as versions of political movements. The politics and culture of the period necessitated the creation of credible belief-systems to resist attack, unite a disparate people, or both. But it was more than just a form of defensiveness. The oneness of a patriarchal Allah seemed the most attractive option, serving to demonstrate the weakness of Christianity and obliterate all links with a polytheistic and matrilineal past. Once again it seemed that whatever the flavor, monotheism could not countenance any other way of being, least of all one that gave women any say in the matter of their own livelihood.

Throughout the rise of monotheism, many of the central tenets of his-story were guiding principles. It was men who became the teachers and leaders, priests and imams. In all cases the *truth*, as it appeared to the respective empires and faiths, was incompatible with that of others. This incompatibility more often than not resulted in armed power struggles and the suppression and violent destruction of anything different. It is an irony that for all the most spiritual verve of Moses, Jesus and Mohammed, the subsequent organization of their teachings has led persistently to bloodshed, war and intolerance. It is a further irony that the similarities between all three monotheistic faiths (the male god, the male prophet, the right-handed work of the written book) have brought the followers closer to war than understanding; symbolized most recently by the battles in Palestine/Israel – a place sacred to all three religions and an example of the difficulty monotheists face in trying to live with each other. It's like the ultimate football match, with supporters armed with guns and missiles, training their children in the laws of combat; no side ready to stop until their team has defeated the others and won the match. It has resulted in atrocious examples of brutality and suffering throughout the last 5,000 years. It is still raging today.

Here Comes the Science

To the rational mind all religion is rubbish. Hearing the voice of god, being healed by touching an old bit of bone, believing in the existence of the soul, are all evidence to the scientific mind of superstition, even insanity. So it might be expected that the 18th century in Europe, with the dawning of the Age of Enlightenment, would shine a light onto the shadows of monotheistic practice, with its priests and gimcrackery, and usher in a new dawn.

A new world there most certainly was. As well as a revolution in science there were revolutions in political thinking. The Age of Reason managed to crowd in on the traditional power bases of regal and ecclesiastical power and, sans culottes, throw them out of court. Instead of priests there were now doctors. Instead of a divinely appointed male aristocracy there were prime ministers and captains of industry. The West had come of age with, as prime-time historian Niall Ferguson has it, a bundle of 'killer apps' that included scientific, political and economic competition.

Unlike the narrative of religion, the scientific story used different language to explain the world. In place of god creating everything there was the Big Bang. Rather than grand design there were random mutations. Instead of seven days there were billions of years. And instead of lords siring future lords, who would rule just because they were lords, there were now men elected by other men, who sat either on one side of a room of the other.

Yet scratch the surface and a story familiar and enduring reveals itself. The dogmas of western science and western politics are as one-sided as the story of religion. Once again they are tales told by men from the self-appointed position of authority, the place of one who knows. In etymology, both the words *science* and *history* have their roots in the phrase 'to know'. Yet what counts as knowledge, and who is permitted to have access to it, remains closely guarded by a gang of boys. As the digital philosopher Sadie Plant observes of the dawning of this 'enlightened' age, 'A small matter of brotherhood, the third great principle of the modern world, guaranteed that human rights were once again the rights of man.'

Perhaps we should be unsurprised to find the solar torch of monotheism burning furiously (now with added facts!) in the fist of science. As historian Jacques Barzun says, science is 'a faith as fanatical as any in history'. Though ruled by accident and evolution, the Enlightenment worldview is as teleological as that of Judaism, Christianity and Islam. First, there is a definite beginning. Rather than divine creation there is a really big explosion, but both display a very masculine perspective. The masculine needs a point of origin to provide not only the premise on which a particular philosophical position is based, but the foundation of that tradition itself. Though it takes the biblical god only seven days as opposed to evolution's incomprehensible eons, the end result is uncannily similar. All these evolving microbes, all the parting of the sea from the land, is only made comprehensible by those men erudite enough to understand the *good* news as the masculine brain speaks it.

For all the talk of revolutions during this period, some key ideas remain unchanged. Look closer and you can see the same story being retold. Copernicus, like Galileo, is often cited with reverence as moving the world out of the dark age of superstition towards the light of reason. He was the first astronomer to formulate a scientifically based heliocentric cosmology that displaced the Earth from the center of the cosmos. Yet in stating that the Earth went round the sun he was doing nothing but echoing Akhenaten who, 3,000 years before him, proclaimed the Sun God as the center of the universe. By turning the Earth into a sycophantic satellite of the solar absolute, his revolution was nothing but a re-instatement of an age-old bias.

The formation of the Royal Society in England, 1660, linked scientific development with a select group of men. The human body, like the natural world, was ready to be dissected by a masculine tool that felt separate enough from the whole to call itself *objective*. Anything that involved women or female power had to be tamed or removed. The potency of laywomen as healers was as discredited by the new medical establishment of science as it had been by the priesthoods of religion. Women were persecuted as witches, their wisdom undermined and mocked as the tales of old wives. The creation of the subsidiary role of nurse, second to the more powerful position of doctor, and for centuries the only position available to women, was another iteration of the millennia-long saga of misogyny.

That women still cannot have their scientific ideas welcomed, taken seriously and explored - even during the late 20th century - can be seen in the example of Elaine Morgan. Her work, exploring the idea that human evolution may have involved a wholly or semi-aquatic stage, has been virulently discredited by a scientific establishment keen to decree who is part of the club and who must be blackballed. Scientists cry 'heresy' at any theories that suggest more holistic interpretations of life, such as Rupert Sheldrake's exploration of Morphic Fields. And when, in 2010, Susan Greenfield was dismissed from her role as director of the Royal Institution (a dismissal that saw the RI settle the case of sexism out of court for an undisclosed sum) justification ranged from attacks on her caliber as a scientist to complaints about her frivolity.

It was another woman, Anita Roddick, who suggested in the 1970s that people might like to have the chance to buy cosmetics that had not been tested on animals. Since the 17th century and the philosophy of René Descartes, most western scientists have treated animals as machines, incapable of experiencing pain and suffering because they lacked the consciousness of humans. The experimentation on and killing of animals in the name of scientific research has grown to the degree that, at the time of writing, between 50 and 100 million vertebrates are used in scientific tests every year. The division between animals and humans, with the lives of the former seen as expendable for the purpose of the latter, has kept animals as fair game to be bred, injected, studied and killed. For all that science may wish itself to be considered different from religion, this assumed superiority looks startlingly similar to the dominion over all animals that man gave himself at the start of *the Bible*.

One of the most popular and radical challenges to the religious story of creation was that provided by Darwinism; the creed most vocally championed by the biologist Richard Dawkins. Darwin's *The Origin of Species* became an overnight best-seller and a bible for scientific evolutionists. In his recent TV program on *The Genius of Charles Darwin*, Dawkins introduced the viewer to his beautiful library and in particular his first edition of Darwin's book. In proclaiming the 'indisputable truth of evolution' is Dawkins doing anything else but following the model of those religious devotees he scorns, by asserting the absolute truth of one man and one book against all others?

A long-standing critic of religion and its prophets, Dawkins entered fully into the ring with his 2006 work *The God Delusion*. He says that, 'Religion makes claims about the universe – the same kind of claims that science makes, except they're usually false.' It's worth noting that he is equally dismissive of any possible shilly-shallying, best-of-both-worlds dualism, reminding the reader, 'It is possible for one side to be completely wrong.'

Like fellow atheist AC Grayling, Dawkins sees himself as in no way similar to those he derides, believing it impossible to overstate the difference between the passionate commitment to biblical fundamentalism and the true scientist's equally passionate commitment to evidence. Yet the more someone insists that only they have sole access to *truth* and *right* (contrary to what anyone else believes), the more they sound like other followers of monotheistic belief systems. Dawkins' desire to smite the unbelievers, using the implacable power of science and reason, is nothing short of the evangelical. As in religion, truth comes across as absolute, and the language of academic success - the triumph of one idea, the destruction of another - seems uncomfortably close to the intolerant language of priests, rabbis and imams. According to Dawkins, 'The scientific view of the world is incompatible with religion ... it is also incompatible with magic ... The scientific world view is true.' But as

fellow scientist Robert Winston points out 'to call a book the God Delusion is very worrying because the title implies that if you don't believe in what I believe then you are "deluded".'

It's a powerful combination that has helped western science to continue the might of masculinity: zealous devotion with indisputable proof. In fact, so powerful is this form of science that it might deserve its own '-ism'. As feminist philosopher Jane Clare Jones defines it, the ideology of 'scientism' involves 'both a claim to authority and a set of metaphysical assumptions. It is the assertion that reality must be understood as a material mechanism and that science is the only legitimate means of describing that reality.'

Of course scientists are as fallibile as anyone else, including priests, but they, as scientist Bart Kosko realized when he wrote *Fuzzy Thinking*, 'could err at the level of logic and math, and they could maintain that error with all the pomp and intolerance of a religious cult'. The ability to see that proof is its own religion is only raised through the mid 20th-century development of Quantum physics, which demonstrates the all too subjective link between the mode of observation and that which is observed. This fuzziness of quantum, with its need to balance the paradox of light as both wave and particle, doesn't make it less scientific; it brings science closer to the ambiguity of the real.

The rational pursuit of political materialism (whether Whig or Tory, communist or capitalist), which arose alongside scientific materialism, also shows the similarities between the new materialist kids on the block and the old monotheistic elites. What remains consistent between the new science and the new politics is the materialism – now *proven* to be all there is. It's as if his-story has literally, with the flicking of the Enlightenment switch, given up the ghost. The ephemeral and ethereal spirit has been exposed as a fake by the self-proclaimed indisputable standards of materialism, and the result, as Jones says, 'of a scientific revolution and the development of liberal political discourse, is the socio-political dominance of capital.'

With the extinction of the soul, capitalism becomes even less balanced than the monotheisms that preceded it. Religion had at least allowed for the existence of a soul - albeit the masculinized version of a Holy Ghost living among the landscape of a single male god and divided world. With the Enlightenment, science arrived and undertook its first major piece of surgery: removing the soul from man as the earlier priests had removed it from women, animals and Nature. The entire cosmos was now soulless: a random string of accidents that happened to make life. Mortality was all we had. There was no divinity, no mystery and no mercy.

By replacing a wobbling moral compass with the rubric of 'survival of the fittest', capitalism saw the chance to make a killing. There's no afterlife, the advert reads, so spend it while you can. Never mind problems of landfill, pollution and waste, which now threaten even capitalism's existence; there's money to be made and what god can rival money in terms of popular appeal? Being loaded is the Holy Grail of capitalism and across mass media its high priests appear in a regular parade, promoting greed, acquisitiveness and envy. Even the sense of ecological crisis doesn't stop the gravy train. No matter how much greenwashing is attempted, capitalism, like every system within this last age, continues to see the Earth as nothing more than a compliant resource to be exploited.

Removing the soul from the world has seen scientific and political materialism in its industry conquer hill, desert and sky, until the planet has been covered in concrete and wrapped with satellites. This was the power of the scientific version of his-story: to give man the freedom to do just as he pleased, but now with a range of highly combustible materials to do it faster. As the economist EF Schumacher wrote, 'From the 17th century science shifted from attempting to understand Nature to focus on her manipulation according to the desires of man.'

Many people believe in capitalism, and with much justification. Surgery removes cancers. Technology generates electricity. Genetically-modified food offers a booming human population the means to sustain itself. Thanks to the military-industrial-pharmaceutical complex that is our modern god, we now live much longer, and resources are ceaselessly poured into efforts to extend the lifespan further. Yet, perversely, this energy seems to have only increased our terror at death and made our lives another aspect of statistics: quantitatively important, with scant regard for quality. To compensate, science and technology give us stuff: more plastic objects and ornaments and fashions than are needed, but that serve a purpose in reinforcing the overwhelmingly materialist worldview. What use is the beauty of Nature when it has no price tag, exclusivity or sense of aspiration? Because science validates only the physical world, it cannot offer us anything else. It can't offer the spiritual gifts of joy, fulfillment and connection, so it indulges us with objects of approximation. We are sold the products that supposedly equate with beauty or the toys that supposedly bring happiness. But, as the French philosopher Luce Irigaray notes, 'By confusing being happy with possessing many goods, we have progressively lost happiness.' Like a busy parent who has no time to spend with their child, gross materialism gives us ever more complex trinkets and plastic toys. And, like children, we find ourselves thrilled by the novelty, vaguely amused and then bored and eager for the next.

As well as making human life easier, capitalism and scientism have given us pollution and waste on a horrific new scale. The ideology of material domination that conquered the world over the last two centuries has encouraged an increasingly destructive behavior towards our environment. Unless we can change this view - to rebalance the clever with the kind - we risk universal destruction. While global temperatures rise, promising changes none of us can predict but most of us now sense, scientism sits in its cardinal pose of absolute certainty, working on ways to interfere still further with the biosphere in the hope that another material invention might provide the remedy. Unfortunately this soulless materialism cannot accept how littered the world already is with the failures of experiments past. As Gaia theorist James Lovelock writes, 'Our continuing development as an intelligent social animal with an ever-increasing dependence upon technology has inevitably disturbed the other living things and will continue to do so.'

Scientism is angrier by the day, confused by the resurgence of people living happily with fewer facts and more feelings; too scared at having to give up its pontiff's throne and hear the question that begins to form on people's lips: whether this impermeable materialism is indeed the answer, or merely the latest incarnation of the problem. Perhaps we need fewer shampoos rather than more.

According to the physicist Stephen Hawking, the future of the human race lies in finding another planet to colonize. Meanwhile, back on planet Earth, we experience a global recession unwitnessed since the American Depression of the 1930s and claiming new victims with each passing day. The solution to the 1930s Depression was Roosevelt's New Deal, which got everyone spending again on public works, borrowing money to revitalize the stagnant economy. The more serious problem for our contemporary system is that we've already maxed out the credit cards and it is clear that the planet cannot sustain much more of this delusional faith in infinite growth. Ongoing rescue packages of quantitative easing have bought the richest pockets of the global financial system a few more years, but they are based on promising more money that doesn't exist and on generating a bezerk faith in the benefits of a bankrupt system that seems more incredible, and more harmful, than the much-berated principle of homeopathy. As people and Nature struggle to be released, people are becoming increasingly aware that keeping capitalism on life-support through increased spending means further harming the life of ourselves and our planet.

Though the absolute authority of religion gave way to western science and political materialism, the motif of imbalance has only increased. The immateriality of a masculine soul was surgically removed by an equally one-sided act of masculine reason. Materialism is very fond of trumpeting its superiority over the militant religions it associates with all things irrational. Yet those arguing for evolution instead of creationism seem to be taking an increasingly fundamentalist attitude befitting the most extreme religious dogmatist. By buying into the latest version of imbalance we have brought about mass pollution and waste that threatens the very future of our species as well as that of every other living being and system on the planet. We have embraced a financial monotheism that has consistently valued greed over compassion, and the accumulation of pointless junk over meaningful experience, on such a scale that even an Iron Lady might turn. We don't need the latest face of L'Oréal to make us ask: is this all we're worth?

Divide and Conquer

Division, as many schoolchildren know, is the moment where maths becomes taxing. There's something innately problematic about splitting things up, and divorce, with the apportioning of crockery and blame, is perhaps the adult example of the suffering that accompanies division. If we want to make things weaker, we split them up. United we stand, as the proverb goes. Divided …

The impulse to split and separate is one of the defining characteristics of this last age. Arguably it began as soon as our trailblazing ancestors began to segregate the land for crops and animals. Its development as an idea was central to biblical and Greek philosophical thought. Not only were man and woman split, and the split accompanied with a moral bias: but more elementally, land was separated from water, light was sundered from dark. As ideas go, the one towards separation had legs.

Greek philosophy gave perhaps the most solid rationale to the concept of separation. Socrates, Plato and Aristotle all worked towards reaffirming the crack in existence between all things. It was Socrates who posited the idea that 'to have pure knowledge of anything, we must get rid of the body' so the soul could become 'separate and independent'. Plato then picked up the pen for his teacher and ran us into a cave, where, as he saw it, we were all prisoners in the dark, watching shadows move on a wall, separated from the *truth* outside in the light which we could never know. By the time Aristotle got his hands on the written word there was no stopping the schism. Everything was observed, described and partitioned, in a magnum opus of separation. Aristotle's binary logic came down to one law: A or not-A: *either* this *or* not this. The problem with this is that any truth moves between total truth and total falsehood. We can put black-and-white labels on things, but the labels will pass from accurate to inaccurate as the things change. But for Aristotle and future thinkers who followed, the boundaries were clear and irreproachable. Genesis might have begun a list of the various life forms man had dominion over, but Aristotle turned it encyclopedic. The vast shelves of *The Encyclopaedia Britannica* present us with the logical outcome of this disease of division, and in the middle of the word itself, the Cyclops, a creature, like the masculine vision, with only one eye.

In the myths and legends of many tribal cultures there are no hard and fast divisions. The world is born into being by a hermaphrodite, one of the greatest conceptual challenges to a worldview that forces things to be *either* this *or* that. Fathers become husbands to their daughters and even creation myths wind out into infinity by having the creator god seeking advice from his mother. While the masculine template might separate trees from rocks according to a list of definitions, in other stories every being, however leafy or stony, is afforded its own spirit, rendering everything unique and connected at the same time. And even widely shared concepts, like the danger of a shark, could be upset by the concept of a familiar (a tutelary spirit in animal form), who would seek out her human friend, rub against his legs in the surf and let him ride on her back.

But for his-story to exist there needed to be strict divisions. So the ancient shamanic concepts of an upper and lower world, equally valid for the practitioner in terms of compassionate spirits offering help in human and animal form, becomes heaven *or* hell, divided by the masculine finger into good *or* bad. When Socrates directed his students out of the cave it was with the following advice: 'You won't go wrong if you connect the ascent into the upper world and the sight of the objects there with the upward progress of the mind into the intelligible region.'

For less philosophical men, this idea of division has had the advantage of separating themselves from the rest of the world and carving it up for their own ends. In *the Qur'an* it is stated that, 'Men have authority over women because Allah has made the one superior to the other.' The rigid statutes that safeguarded such inequality were zealously preserved. For the indigenous cultures that found themselves on the receiving end of this pejorative split they faced a move to categorize the world according to western paradigms, which led to the erasure of vital stories about their way of life as *primitive* and *mistaken*. So the story of the origin of the Native Americans became the scientific fact of migration from the Siberian Triangle at the time of the last ice age. Not everyone was happy about this, not least the Native Americans, who hadn't even been consulted about their own origin accounts. Winston Churchill refused to condemn the process of division and conquest during the Peel Enquiry of 1937. He said,

> I do not admit … that a great wrong has been done to the Red Indians of America, or the black people of Australia. I do not admit that a wrong has been done to these people by the fact that a stronger race, a higher grade race, a more worldly-wise race, to put it that way, has come in and taken their place.

When Hitler led Germany into war two years later and launched one of the most defining examples of dominance through division, the Holocaust, it was with supreme personal rule that he kept his subordinates divided.

Value judgments associated with this principle of division could be summoned when the mood, or the chance of profit, presented itself. So a patron of the 18th-century artist Brunais described the Carib descendants of shipwrecked African slaves in the West Indies as 'quiet and well-disposed'. When he discovered they occupied the windward side of the island, ideal for sugar cultivation, and would not cede it to British colonists, they became *Black* Caribs and were judged to be 'ignorant, savage, lawless, distrustful and cunning'.

As the stories of experiences on the other side of this divide swell and return, it becomes easier to witness this pattern over thousands of years, but for most of this age the pen describing the split has been in the hands of the very people benefiting from it. History, as the adage goes, is written by the victors. And throughout this age the spoils that came from such division must have appeared giddying. Who would complain when, in place of hunting, animals could be farmed and sold? Who minded when, in place of an uncertain world at the end of which ego-death loomed, there was now a son and heir to take over and continue the family line? Who else, but the people and life forms for whom his-story denied a voice.

Hierarchy is a powerful model. Many revolutionaries have attempted to turn the world upside down, only to find it falling back to Earth in a pretty similar pyramidal shape, but with different people in charge. Abraham Maslow's behavioral model of the Hierarchy of Needs demonstrates that Nature provides its own pyramid, with the need for air coming before the need for water and both before the need for earth (food) and fire. There are hierarchies of need and there are hierarchies of value in a pack of cards. There is a king of the jungle and there is always a queen bee. The archetype of Queen and King is older than Adam, and the presence of the two models of human sex, with their relative strengths and weaknesses, can be seen on any chess-board.

But this age has not played fair with the innate concept of leadership, writing in the rulebook that the status and wealth of the father go straight to the eldest son. This position of inherited entitlement, found within hereditary peers and monarchs is, as Thomas Paine said, 'as absurd a proposition as a hereditary doctor or mathematician.' But across the social spectrum and down the centuries, the rule of hereditary inheritance links men dividing the spoils of the world with other men. It is how patri-archy supports itself. It's almost as if it says, 'Keep things going this way, my son, and you can inherit the lot.' It is noticeable in bloodlines across the world, named after the preceding male and evidenced by the mass of *sir*-names for every Thomson, Dickson and Harrison. Patrilineal descent is the model that links the spiritual, political and personal. Under the logic of his-story, hereditary kingship was bestowed upon the king by god. This was the dominant theory underpinning, for example, medieval monarchs in Europe, unless they were too feminine (in which case the lords temporal made sure to lock them up, torture and kill them, as with Richard II, William Rufus and Edward II). It implied that god himself was the ultimate lad in this vast *Boys' Own* adventure. The pattern, most often called feudal, is essentially patriarchal. It applies as much to Roman emperors as capitalist CEOs, extends to all political organizations and finds its most intimate setting within the family. 'Head of the Household' is a title that, even today, helps many men to see themselves as above their wives and children.

One of the most consistent aspects of the on-going division upheld by hereditary rule is the way it has repeatedly denied women. From the earliest years the rise in male power came at the direct expense of others, and women were the biggest losers. Enshrined by codes and biblical law, the story of woman has been of servitude to the father followed by servitude to the husband. The privileged place held by men in economic life, their social usefulness, the prestige of marriage, the value of masculine backing – all enslaved women to the bidding of men. If a woman married she immediately became the possession of her husband where the marriage oath 'to honor and obey' was sealed by a band of gold. Until the 1980s it was not considered legally possible for a man to rape his wife, such were the *rights* of the husband. If a father had only a female child his estate went to the next surviving male relative. As Virginia Woolf wrote of her transgender hero/ine Orlando, 'The chief charges against were (1) that she was dead, and therefore could not hold any property whatsoever; (2) that she was a woman, which amounts to much the same thing.' Whether gavelkind or primogeniture, women were consistently bypassed, sold off and used as barter. Whether it's Elizabeth I excusing her sex or Mary Ann Evans taking the moniker George Eliot to ensure publication, his-story has repeatedly relegated women to the footnotes. As Jane Austen wrote, 'Men have had the advantage of us in telling their own story. Education has been theirs in so much higher a degree; the pen has been in their hands.'

One of the simplest examples of this enduring schism between the masculine and feminine is with two numbers: zero and one. In schoolrooms across the world it is still taught that zero is less than one. At an early age, boys are encouraged to see their phallic digit as proof of something against the absence of a girl's hole. And the fact that girls were supposed to see the same was thoroughly theorized by Freud. Girls naturally had penis envy. Boys could never have womb envy. To be zero was to be deficient, empty, redundant, lacking. In mathematics, zero counted for nothing and an infinite string of zeros could only be made valuable by the inclusion of some positive male one.

Nowhere has the converse been taught. That zero can be everything: that the circle of zero is the entirety of a pie from which fractions are cut; that the circle is the wheel of planets, seasons and stars; is the cycle of time from life to death to rebirth. Nowhere could the one-sided absolutism of a world where things were *either* one thing *or* another embrace the paradox of zero: that it could be both everything and nothing at the same time. Nowhere could the hole be the whole.

More than just reclaiming the potencies of zero, there is the on/off symbol, silently waiting on each form of modern technology, where the zero is combined with the one. Unlike the way mathematics has been taught throughout this last age, digital technology reminds us that everything we see and hear on our screens is composed of nothing but a sequence of zeroes and ones. Zero is not less than one, it is on par, capable of being everything and nothing at the same time, mystical and paradoxical and vital. Together, male and female, masculine and feminine, yin and yang – all the dualities imaginable – can coalesce and harmonize.

Like zero, the circle makes its dominance and weakness felt together in the pack of cards. Rather than the monarchic superiority of King and Queen, it is the ace that trumps everything. An androgynous shape-shifter, a trickster (like the fool in the tarot pack), the ace is as mercurial as the spiraling circle that goes on without beginning or end. It is ridiculous and triumphant, both the lowest of the low and the highest of the high, changing between the two without alteration. It is a seamless link that brings the feminine circle back to begin again. It is everything and nothing and its centrality, mistress, mastery and mischief is where we find ourselves again now.

And in terms of power, the presence of ambiguous zero is vital if, rather than continued division, we might like to enjoy a spell of inclusion. Only when zero is factored in positively can we see ourselves as part of a bigger story, not trapped in a struggle between two divided opposites. Only when we sit in circle are we allowed to be different, equal and valid aspects of everything. Division means we know only imbalance. Holism brings us round to tolerance, allows each of us space, makes us feel a little bit smaller.

To be happy with this smallness, whether standing before an ocean or looking up at the sky, to be comfortable with vulerability, is difficult to feel if there's an established tradition of division. Division increases fear and the need to get the upper hand. It sees difference as dangerous. It tries to take control, shackle other peoples, neuter other species and forbid their practices; force them to convert or die. And this division, this us *or* them mentality, can be linked with the intensive farming of animals, the mass destruction of ecosystems and the damage to our own beings. If we see others as separate from us rather than part of the whole, it becomes easier to dissociate from what happens to them. There is very little during this age that has not been burnt, crushed, shot, bullied, raped, drowned, cut, banished, vanquished and silenced because of this unfettered masculine tendency to divide.

The well-managed system of perpetual hierarchal rule has ensured that only the complicit few have come close to sharing power with the leaders. In a brutal contest, power has been physically wrestled by the strongest and most aggressive, irrespective of other talents of leadership, even when such violence means, as Macbeth intuited, that 'blood will have blood'. Julius Caesar made war on the senate until he became Emperor, only to be stabbed in the side and front as well as the back. The concept of division that promised so much to the lucky few had one particular drawback. In actively seeking to reduce the attention paid to the different and many, by neglecting to include everyone equally in the circle, there was going to be trouble ahead. The riches went to the men who were most physically strong, violent and organized, but the other blokes weren't going to go down without a fight. One of the earliest and most lasting partners to 5,000 years of division is conflict.

Let the games commence …

Battle Fatigues

'History,' as Rudge remarks in Alan Bennett's play *The History Boys*, 'is just one fucking thing after another.' The exhaustion is understandable. There's a growing sense that this age of division, and its legacy of dispute, bloodshed and war, is beginning to pall.

In trying to think of an example of *battle* the task is made difficult by the surfeit of choices. Shall we be historic and opt for the *Battle of the Somme* or be retro and go for *Battle of the Planets*? What about the *Doctor Who* gaming cards, *Battles in Time*, or shall we bring it to the cinema with *Battle: Los Angeles*? How about being geographic and going for the site near Hastings where the Normans met the English and which for almost a thousand years has been known simply as *Battle*?

Ideologically, we've been fighting the battle for truth, people battle for freedom and more than one skirmish has been undertaken as a battle for peace. There are pitch battles and battles for custody; crowded shopping excursions requiring us to battle through town and battle for parking spaces while all the time waging the battle of the sexes. We have wars on terror, on drugs, on crime, on germs, on poverty. There are robot wars, star wars, price wars. When did being alive require such perpetual conflict?

A list of wars and battles isn't just excessive in history: it *is* his-story. Cain and Abel were the first biblical siblings, for whom brotherly love meant one killing the other. Later, when Remus failed to agree on his brother's preferred spot for the foundation of Rome, Romulus killed him. And on it's gone. Ironically, for all the attempts of organized religion to rouse spiritual devotion, religious wars have been and continue to be the form of conflict that most devastates the world.

If something is worth fighting for it's supposed to have importance. The end justifies the means and whatever destruction and loss of life, civilian and military, on either side, is chalked up as necessary. To fight is seen as brave, to lay down weapons weak. To fight for *truth* and vanquish *lies* once again makes absolute enemies. 'We are the *good* guys – it's the others who are in the *wrong*,' both sides seem to repeat without hearing the echo.

According to military historians the first armies we know about existed from about 2500 BC in the city-states of Sumer in Southern Mesopotamia. It can't be disputed that warfare has been central to the development of our culture, with so many empires forging their version of civilization through war. But there is some dispute over whether the existence of war is eternal or located purely in the age where men have been in charge. Some suggest that by undertaking ritualized forms of combat in performance and dance, other cultures have minimized the need for casualties. Among the Semai of Malaysia, the military practices of ritual and symbolic combat resolve conflict with little killing and sometimes without bloodletting at all. In eastern martial arts the aim of combat is to develop skills, not to amass the biggest body count. Our world has strayed from this idea so far that the greatest destruction now rests on a small red button any fool could press.

While some geneticists argue that war is an evolutionary trait that favors the strong, others suggest something different. Controversial anthropologist Margaret Mead offered her discoveries of life in the non-violent island culture of Samoa as evidence that war is an invention, not a biological necessity. The prehistoric prevalence of human sacrifice and hunting might also explain how the masculine energy of focused assault could have been let with more balance. But the rule of men during this age, with division of land and property and peoples, has led to a prevalence of war. What began around 5,000 years ago in Mesopotamia has grown in stature and complexity, in financial, ecological and emotional cost, to become the enemy of human life. It is ironic that, as military historian John Keagan says,

> automatic weapon fire, massed artillery bombardment, aerial bombing, unpiloted missiles and ultimately nuclear and thermonuclear weapons – almost every single one of the [20th] century's so-called advances in military technology or practice – was conceived and developed as a means of sparing loss of life.

In trying to avoid death we seem to have done nothing so much as brought it about.

Five thousand years is a long rail from which to pick a pertinent blood-stained garment, so let's content ourselves with the last century, a time when the exponential increase in the human population across the world has been matched by a similar advance in the capacity for destruction.

In 1914 the power and wealth of the major countries in Europe was enormous, and the colonial division of the rest of the world at their hands was akin to a table of greedy diners carving up slabs of meat between themselves. As green eyes flickered at the quantities on other dishes, so the leaders panicked about the safety of their own colonial riches. Treaties were drawn up promising mutual assistance, the occupants of the table took sides and the matter of a Serbian nationalist shooting Franz Ferdinand, heir to the Austro-Hungarian Empire, was the trigger that brought first Russia, then Germany, then France and Britain into conflict. The Great War began in Britain like a Royal Wedding, with bunting on the street, celebrations and a sense of relief. By 1918 the landscape was changed. Thirty seven million people had died as a result of a war that had not been glorious and swift but long and bloody.

Nor was it, as Lloyd George hoped, 'the war to end all wars'. The Second World War lasted from 1939 to 1945 and when 1945 arrived it did so in the same way that the second act of a play closes: with the suggestion at the nature of the third. The atomic bomb, developed by European scientists for nuclear energy to power our fast-advancing culture, exploded in Hiroshima and Nagasaki in Japan. The televised plume of a mushroom cloud was a spectacular nightmare to close one war and herald the next. The Cold War lasted for the next 40 years, dwarfed by the continual threat of nuclear devastation recurring anywhere in the world. This time the obligatory two sides of conflict were capitalist and communist. Though the most famous localized battle of this war scarred the land and peoples of Vietnam and spurred on the peace movement of the 1960s, it was a war fought more on the threat of war. Like a protracted out-staring competition, moments like the Bay of Pigs crisis in 1962 tested the American and Soviet power blocs to see who would blink first. And in 1989, when the Berlin Wall came down and communism collapsed as an ideological power in the USSR and Eastern Europe, capitalism was declared the victor and the world hissed open a can of coke.

Only another seed had dropped from the Second World War. Horrified by the extent of the genocide of the Jewish people in Nazi Germany, pressure grew to find a piece of land for the displaced people. The state of Israel was officially launched in 1948, though there was less thought given to the livelihood of the Palestinians already living there and none for the 700,000 who were elbowed out of their homes and communities to make way for the new arrivals. The concept of sharing the land disappeared in a riot of bullets and as Islam became more defiant after the Suez crisis in 1956, and in the face of Israel gaining nuclear weapons from Britain and America in the 1960s, so the people of a disputed territory embarked on a bitter, relentless conflict still unresolved at the time of writing.

For all those who believed organized religion had sunk into irrelevance, the destruction of the Twin Towers in New York was a reminder that the feuding of different belief systems, which propelled us repeatedly into battle over the last five millennia, was as present at the end of this age as it had been at the start.

After 2001 fundamental positions were drawn. George Bush was no longer just the commander-in-chief of the American armed forces. He was also a devout Christian hearing the voice of god telling him to bomb Iraq and marshalling once again the Wild West rhetoric of goodies *versus* baddies; declaring war on terror and war on the 'Axis of Evil'. Across the Islamic states of Iraq and Iran, powerful Shia elites made clear that this was *Jihad*, a Holy War against the godless west, with their petro-dollars and bloodied colonial hands. Saddam Hussein, the one-time ruler of Iraq (supported in the 1980s by America against the revitalized Islamic elite led by Ayatollah Khomeini in Iran), was violently removed from power in 2003 and executed 3 years later. Yet the 'liberation' of Iraq has not ushered in peace. Bombings from London to Madrid to Mumbai remind us that this particular war has not fully receded, if indeed it has even started.

Karen Armstrong writes that, 'One of the most startling developments of the late 20th century has been the emergence within every major religious tradition of a militant piety popularly known as "fundamentalism".' This recent growth of fundamentalism, playing out a final act by returning the world's attention to where this very age began, with images of babies armed with bombs and toddlers taught to handle guns, feels as necessary as it does ghastly. It's almost like the circularity of the narrative has to be honored, lest we ever, genuinely, forget. Traditionally, times of stress and change encourage more extreme forms of behavior. Factions and groups, on local, national or pan-national levels, seem to sense impending change and, as they do so, develop religions of hate. Fundamentalism is not just the preserve of one sect. The clerics in Iran who favor extreme interpretations of *the Qur'an*, like Pastor Terry Jones in America who judged the holy book before burning it, are reflections of each other and of a wider hostility. Even once-pacific Buddhists and Hindus are arming themselves and the proponents of cool, dispassionate science are becoming belligerent. Everywhere it seems the temperature is hotting up.

Maybe the warming of the climate finds its human mirror in the heating of passions. If an awareness of this longstanding narrative of the inherent battle of his-story is coming to consciousness, it may be much to the planet's relief. Maybe it's only by engaging with the underlying story of conflict – across tribes and parties, through religious and material belief systems - and appreciating its root in unbalanced masculinity, that will complete it, allowing for other, more inclusive and harmonious, stories to be told.

The Olympics started in 2008 in Beijing the same day as Russia set upon Georgia for attacking South Ossetia. As a celebration of global gaming began, footage of tanks and casualties provided stark contrast. If we are truly to tire of war but still enjoy the spirit of games and competitions we could do worse than consider what happens at school when we take sides without coming back together after. The prevalence of competition, on the pitch, in the classroom and across capitalism, is endemic. But if we separate into sides without rejoining, we are liable to continue teaching his-story where everything in life is a battle. If we don't make a circle to begin and end with, then bitterness and division carry on unmended. Undissolved, they heap up, day after day, promoting rivalry, out of which conflicts become unrelenting and merely another twist in the angry battle to hit back, until the start of the quarrel is barely remembered. In its place is the stinging sense of vengeance that seeks to land the final, fatal punch. We have demonstrated our differences through conflict with superb clarity. We need more than ever to remember what knits us back together.

On the side of the temple at Angkor Wat, Cambodia, there is a carved relief entitled 'The Churning of the Milky Ocean'. It shows two opposing snakes coming from different sides to blend the elixir of the world together. The first people who taste it and soar through the air are the dancers; finding ways, like in

Brazilian *Capoeira,* to move with grace, ease, flow and style; allowing battle to become ballet.

It is one thing to mark out a pitch in order to play a game. It is something else to have institutionalized division across the world until the very playing field itself is threatened with destruction. We all have the birthright of differing beliefs, ideas and experiences. We all have bad-hair days, get mad and want to smash something up. But unless we find ways to come together in circle and express our anger rather than direct it, unless we heal, practice tolerance and hear others as we ourselves want to be heard, we will continue to inflict great pain on the world and each other. There is no problem in picking sides to play, as long as we don't forget to unpick them after.

Organized brutality arose from the Ancient world, crossed the Medieval and entered the Modern. It drove invasions, revolutions and usurpations throughout the centuries, up to the genocides of the 20th century and beyond. The only place where women and children came first was in order of suffering. In every other respect they were an afterthought. Every wife and daughter and sister whose appearance in the unrelenting and bloody struggle of page after page of his-story has been, as Mrs. Lintott summarized in *The History Boys,* 'women following behind with the bucket'.

To find our way out of this we need to turn to the stories that have been dwarfed and ignored. We need to return to the heart of the home, to feminine tales and our mothers' tongues.

Watch out, boys: the political just got personal.

Cheating at Eating

Gillian McKeith's rubric 'You are what you eat' is one of those old wise tales so obvious it seems inane to reproduce. Ancient, pagan tribes long ago grasped the simple equation that what we consume we become; that our diet determines the shape of us. For nomadic cultures the easiest recipe was to eat what grew or grazed nearest, straight from the earth and full of life force. Conversing with the spirits of plants and trees helped them learn what food did what. For most of us, we've moved so far from a direct relationship with the land that our food is processed and packaged at unknown locations, untold hundreds of miles away. The apple that began his-story sowed a seed of suspicion that germinated: that Nature was out to get us and must be treated with chemicals or else.

Tribal societies that undertook hunting animals made a sacred ritual out of the pursuit. The power of ingesting an animal was understood to be enormous and courting it to die for people to live no less so. Catching, cooking and eating involved honoring Animal and Nature (both physical and spiritual) by consuming food together in celebration and gratitude at a pace that ensured healthy digestion. Every part of the animal was used (skin, flesh, gut and bone) and, like the natural order, nothing was wasted. For many of us, our experience of food now is something to hurry through, convenient and fast, with no regard for either the quality of the dish, its ingredients and preparation or even its meaning. Moving faster, we eat on the trot. Food is suctioned rather than chewed and with scarcely an afterthought at what to do with the conveniently disposable, though damagingly resilient, plastic packaging. Meanwhile awareness grows of the need somehow to return to a more sustainable and sustaining diet. Not so much the wistful dream of a simple life, as a realization of how central food is to the whole living scheme of things. The price of food, both financial and nutritional, is nothing less than a matter of life and death.

The first steps away from the hunting stage were the beginnings of agriculture and the domestication of animals. The movement from a nomadic co-existence with Nature led to the partitioning of land and ownership and the marking of boundaries and enclosures. 'Old McDonald's Farm', sung across nurseries and infant schools, tells a tale of the land that it was always thus. The farmer always dug up his fields, seeds were sown, the land was cultivated and crops were harvested. More recently, McDonald's has become a global brand whose golden arches straddle continents, whose need for ever-increasing pasture land involves continued deforestation and whose now ubiquitous beef burgers arrived in the UK at a time when cows went mad when fed on a macabre diet of their own crushed relatives. This agricultural system that now produces most of the world's food supply (favoring the rich few over the poor many) developed at a point in time. Far from being the eternal way of peoples, like the flowering of plants and the swing of the tides, the inception of agriculture marks the beginning of his-story. It has formed the staple diet through which our system, with its greed and inequality, has swelled.

The husband (and the act of husbandry) made chattels of women, animals and land alike. The balance that once existed between the hunters and gatherers was replaced by a growing theory of property with a man as the household's head. As agriculture spread, so too did the equation of land as a source of revenue and power. The more land you owned (or fought for, or stole, or conquered), the more resources you had at your disposal and the wealthier you were. Over ensuing millennia the amount of wilderness shrank and forests were decimated to make way for farmland. The trend towards enclosing land became an issue of contention in England when the open field system (with common land to be enjoyed, foraged over and grazed on by all) was increasingly taken into private hands. By the 16th century the commons were being seized unilaterally by landowners to make way for the grazing of privately owned sheep. The issue of enclosures marked many of the social rebellions of the time and, in his *Utopia*, the Tudor writer and politician Thomas More suggested a link between the rise in enclosures and the increase in theft and social problems. One of the first victims of the boom in agriculture remains so to this day: trees.

Deforestation is becoming a recognized problem but, despite the rising awareness among groups of environmentalists, it is not a serious concern to the engines of global capital, following the millennia-old pattern of taking what they like to fulfill 'man's needs'.

Successive generations plowing this furrow of private ownership have only become better skilled at taking from the land what they want. Whether wheat, potatoes and tobacco or metal, coal and oil, the process has remained the same as the one Joseph Conrad describes in *Heart of Darkness*, undertaken by European colonists in Africa: 'To tear treasure out of the bowels of the land was their desire, with no more moral purpose at the back of it than there is in burglars breaking into a safe.' But the intensity of technological development in use since the Industrial Revolution has enabled the mines to go deeper, the drilling to be faster, the swathes of ocean bed to be more ubiquitously harvested. And the more people who benefit from mass agriculture, the larger the human population and the further the extent of such reaping required to sustain us. As Carol Ann Duffy observes in her poem 'Work', 'To feed one, she worked from home', but

> A billion named,
> she trawled the seas, hoovered fish, felled trees,
> grazed beef, sold cheap fast food, put in
> a 90 hour week.

Profits and productivity now determine the nature of modern food production, and mass monoculture is viewed as necessary to feed over 6 billion people. All these human mouths need satisfying and the underlying expectation is that we have the right to eat as much of what we like when we like. It is a luxury we have come to regard as necessary for our survival. But it is a policy from teaspoon to trawler that brings with it, in the words of Al Gore, 'an unprecedented and massive collision between our civilization and the earth'.

Then there is the way certain key ingredients have found their way repeatedly onto our plates. The mass ingestion of sugar, chocolate and potatoes can be traced back to the Trade Winds carrying European colonists, from the 17th century onwards, via the slave ports of West Africa to the newly *owned* lands of the Americas. The nutritional value of these commodities was low, but they provided a cheap source of energy that contributed to European industrialization. It is the same combination of sugars, caffeine and starches that we rely on for energy today. Fattening and decaying such food may be, but it is financially cheap, compulsive and essential for the massive amounts of speedily released energy our fast-paced world demands. It is little surprise that sugared chocolate and chemically enhanced potato chips are the dominant fuel available at petrol stations, next to petrol itself.

If we take the McMeal as the barometer for our global diet, we find sugar, starch, meat and salt with a near absence of anything green, raw or recently picked. Our pattern of food growing and consuming has led us to a point where we are regularly poisoning ourselves and queuing up for seconds. Morgan Spurlock's film *Supersize Me!* showed the legacy of physical and mental ill health that comes from such an entrenched diet. While it is increasingly known that fast and industrially processed foods are responsible for the enormous growth in the number of overweight people in contemporary society, the McMeal remains the staple of those too poor, exhausted and excluded to cultivate a different menu. The cheapest way to get a 100-calorie intake is to buy fats, processed starches and sugars. If our diets tell us who we are, the results are a litany of imbalance and powerlessness. Food has become a source of anxiety, with food allergies and intolerances growing alongside the extremes of obesity and anorexia. Natural food that does, quite literally, grow on trees, is left to rot; feared by those of us who have not been taught what can and can't be eaten; scarily raw to our modern tastes that demand our produce preserved and packaged. 'All this manipulation of our senses has led us into a diet that is good for profits but damages our health,' observes nutritional writer Felicity Lawrence. 'The genius of contemporary globalised capitalism has been not just that it gives consumers what they want but that it is able to make them want what it has to sell.' To encourage us to exercise and engage more intimately with the land, to allow the fruits to grow harmoniously and in their own time, appears laughable to a money-driven system. Where's the profit in helping people take what they need for free?

James Lovelock says, 'Only when we think of our planetary home as if it were alive can we see why farming abrades the living tissue of its skin and why pollution is poisonous to it as well as to us.' And the movement to return to the Earth is growing. Books like botanist Richard Mabey's *Food for Free* remind us that Nature instinctively provides in abundance what works on her terrain. The Transition Movement, as given voice by Bob Hopkins, offers suggestions for ways out of oil-dependency towards local and sustainable growth and reforestation; pitching our hope of survival at recognizing ourselves as symbiotic creatures who need to live with the rest of the planet. The movement is young and five millennia of imbalance incredibly ingrained. But the emergence of Transition Towns in the UK, like Totnes and Lewes, and Kinsale in Eire, provides a positive sense that the need for adaptation is widely felt and socially as well as environmentally empowering. Rising food costs expose the lie that agro-industry is cheaper than local and organic food, and meat farming is revealed as being a serious contributor to heart disease, obesity, deforestation and rising methane levels.

The challenge is for us to take steps as volunteers of the new way (that is paradoxically the old way) before the eco-system we depend upon forces us. Personal choice and responsibility will count because the multinational companies would not exist if we had not demanded their products and at a price that makes them produce without care for the consequences. Living dislocated in urban settings and expecting nourishment from pre-packaged, machine-made food is like waiting for inspiration from a radiator. High definition plasma screens may entertain us, but when the chips are done, you can't eat an Apple Mac.

To value our selves means valuing the planet. To nourish our beings means nourishing the Earth. What bottom-up, socially inclusive projects like the Transition Movement cherish, and what the imbalanced globalized and homogeneous system does not, is the vitality of the smallest and apparently weakest ingredient. Despite having the world on a plate, we would do well to heed the welfare of something as physically small as the bee.

The Buzz

Much is made of the bees disappearing. News has filtered out of the minor columns of newspapers and esoteric emails to become a global quandary, highlighted by the 2010 United Nations Environment Programme on emerging issues. Together with the sense of sentimental loss comes something else: a reminder from Albert Einstein that if the bees were to disappear, mankind would have four years left on the planet. This isn't just because the human race has a chronically overdeveloped sweet tooth, but because of the enormous amount of crops dependent on the work of the bee for pollination.

It's a sobering time scale and brings our fantastic musings of civilized life in 90, 50, even 20 years' time back to earth. It's akin to the studies of ice melt in the Arctic. In 2007 the Intergovernmental Panel on Climate Change issued a report that projected the disappearance of ice from the Arctic sea by the end of the 21st century. But it seems that the melting is happening far faster than that and some predict the melting of sea ice as soon as 2013. One of the factors slowly dawning on scientists and model makers is the complexity of feedback mechanisms, meaning the ways in which already existent changes work to speed up the process to rapid non-linear collapse. With Einstein's four-year lag we are reminded of the interconnectedness of the Earth's feedback mechanisms and are invited to bravely accept we may be underestimating the extent of the changes facing us and overstating the amount of time we have left to continue functioning as we are.

We like bees. Unlike wasps they are not at liberty to sting indefinitely, and their busy wanderings through the blossoming meadows of summer have a very tangible and appealing end product. Bees make honey and honey is sweet, therefore there is something sweet about bees. The bumblebee goes further to ensure our affections, mocking physical laws by being an aerodynamic impossibility. If our relationships with insects can sometimes see fear bordering on the pathological, bees buzz in to rescue us. They're even furry!

Other life forms have suffered as a result of his-story. The dodo was a victim of the Dutch colonists who settled on the island of Mauritius in the 16th century and brought with them pigs and macaques that truffled and ate all the birds' eggs. Being flightless in paradise had never been a disadvantage, until the settlers changed the rules. In a 2006 survey by the World Conservation Union it was estimated that 40% of all organisms are now endangered, including creatures like the blue whale, snow leopard and tiger: far less open to ridicule than the dear old dead dodo.

But bees offer us more than just an example of how another species might flounder because of our unswerving determination to drive our planet off the road. The way bees have been managed exemplifies the way we have determined our own settled, agricultural way of life. It demonstrates the need of this last age to control and order Nature rather than exist symbiotically and harmoniously with her. It reflects the cost of his-story and reminds us that in a closed system like Gaia, with interdependent parts, every thought, word and deed has a result.

Left to their own devices, honeybees swarm in hollows of rocks and trees. They stay and build a hive of comb in mesmerizing and waste-negating hexagons. There are the dandified male drones, eschewing work to become suitors for the young princesses; the female workers that bring about the prosperity of the colony; and one queen, who in her solitary dignity carries the fate of all. The process of pollination helps both the bees and the plants and flowers they visit. When it's time, they swarm and leave for elsewhere. It's a happy reality that leaves a myriad of useful by-products. For those who traditionally kept bees, the practice was one of harmony. Honey, wax, propolis and pollen were undoubtedly beneficial, but many kept bees out of curiosity, providing a warm, dark enclave for them while understanding that at any time they might depart. For centuries beekeeping, and the Path of Pollen that accompanied it, was seen as one of those occult practices, veiled (literally, for protection) and smudged with smoke.

But the masculine way that ordered agriculture, demanding that people settle and making settlers out of animals, had designs on bees. Bees were no longer left to roam according to their own fancies, but were provided first with skeps, then in 1851 (thanks to Mr. Langstroth) with the movable hive. Now in our globalized age, bees have been set to work. The growing taste for sugar has sweetened our palates, and the need to pollinate vast orchards to satisfy the consumption of growing numbers of humans takes the fabled industry of the bee and makes it do overtime. Like Protestantism and its associated work ethic, which took hold in Northern Europe and became the dominant religion in North America, our treatment of bees mirrors the way we treat and allow ourselves to be treated. Like us, bees have been devalued, kept in multiple boxes in close confinement, made to work for someone else's benefit, having their natural gift removed and replaced with artificial sweeteners.

Working as hard as this, it's not long before both people and bees start dropping. No one is sure why Colony Collapse Disorder is spreading in America and Europe. Among the suggested reasons are electromagnetic radiation, viruses, mites and reactions to chemicals and pathogens. One of the ideas, discussed by Alison Benjamin and Brian McCallum in *A World Without Bees*, concerns the abnormal rates at which bees are now made to work under monoculture's system of contract pollination: being shipped from almond plantation to apple orchard to blueberry farm across America, without time to rest (and dream), at a pace crippling to the health of the immune system.

But it is in the combination of factors that the scale of the problem is revealed. They write:

> We have seen honeybees treated more like machines than animals … how selection has created honey-making automata that are poorly adapted to their living conditions, and ill-equipped to fight off disease. We have discovered how western honeybees have endured crisis after crisis ever since humans took them to far-flung places where parasites were waiting to pounce … We have heard how honeybees have been carelessly killed by pesticides … Environmental changes, from urbanization to rising temperatures and the spread of monocultural agriculture, have made the honeybees' diet less nutritious, and weakened their defense mechanisms.

It's a longstanding and entangled problem but the strap line for CCD might easily read, 'If we treat animals like machines then we shouldn't be surprised when they break down.'

Beekeeper and author Simon Buxton agrees that the problem is human-made and traces it back centuries before pollination management and the Varroa virus.

> The seed of the problem goes back to working with bee skeps. The only way of extracting honey was to kill the bees using sulphur. Obviously you couldn't kill all the bees and the hives that were killed were those with the most honey. They killed the strongest, repeating it year after year until it persistently weakened the strain.

If one word sums up this persistent shortsightedness it is *greed*. 'It's all about squeezing the last drop of honey from the hive, the last drop of milk from the udder, the last drop of oil from the land,' says Buxton:

> It's the same story. We are leading an assault on the structure of the planet and the intricate ecological jigsaw is coming apart. The great metabolic processes of the earth, like pollination and photosynthesis, the synergy of all life that gives shape to all other narratives like religion, myth and science, are coming apart. The very story of Earth is unraveling.

Einstein also said, 'Seeing with eyes of wholeness means recognizing that nothing occurs in isolation, that problems need to be seen within the context of whole systems.' It is estimated that a third of human food supply depends on insect pollination, most of which is accomplished by bees. Even if bees were not central to the pollination of so many crops we happily tuck into on a daily basis, their disappearance should be a powerful step in the ever-mounting pile of evidence asking us to put down our tools before we are made to. One of the rising diseases of the fast-paced modern world is ME or chronic fatigue. Such exhaustion means we are physically prevented from doing even the simplest tasks and become vulnerable to diseases that our immune systems would have once robustly deflected. As with people, so with the world. We court environmental collapse because we see our planet as nothing more than a creature to be flogged to death.

Wherever the bees are going, it's almost certainly not back to work.

Speed the Plow

Today I'm sick. It's just a cold: that small insolvable illness that makes you want to crawl into bed and rest. Outside I can hear the engine of society motor on; a dual carriageway, cars shifting gears uphill, those incessant sirens that suggest city living is a near constant state of emergency. Happily enough it's only a cold. I'll rest and give it the folk duration I was taught by my grandmother (four days to come, four days to stay, four days to go). It will pass. Less a threat than a reminder I need to stop.

For many of us, taking time off to heal is a cause for guilt. We are told not to let our bodies stand in our way. Adverts sell us everything from headache tablets to bowel control in an effort to keep us up and busy living the white-smiled life of the models acting in them. The machine needs its cogs functioning at optimum through day and night, irrespective of weather or season. And if we experience indigestion, nausea, aches or pains, we are directed to the pharmaceutical drugs that numb them.

The ability to embrace vulnerability and mortality has not been encouraged during this age. Crying in women has often been considered a sign of the curse of the female sex, like hysteria: a word coined by men to apply as description, explanation and gag to those with a womb. Crying in men has been reprimanded from birth. Similarly sickness has been considered a feminine affliction, the incapacity to cope with the rigors of a man-made life. Sensitivity, delicacy and softness have fared ill under a myopic age where only the physically fit win the race.

Empire, whether under Alexander, Caesar, Charlemagne or Queen Victoria, has demanded exertion. Rome mightn't have been built in a day but nor did the foremen allow long lunches, siestas and days off. It takes a lot of effort to transform the surface of the world as humankind has done over the last 5,000 years. This kind of building program doesn't happen through napping.

Despite the mass construction of cathedrals during the medieval period, Europe maintained enough of its pagan roots to keep work in check. Seasons were observed and celebrated, the work of spring and harvest offset by the playful summer and hibernatory winter. It wasn't just witches who were following the pattern of the pagan festivals. The Fathers of the Christian religion supplanted its festivities onto those ancient holy days to make it more popular. Though the old feast and fast days were renamed 'saint's days', to redirect people's attentions and thoughts to Christianity, there were (according to *Old Hawkin's Almanac* of 1521) around 140 holy days and 48 market and ember days per year, providing days of sacred observation, during which nothing resembling work could take place. This meant roughly one day of dancing, festivity, contemplation, abstinence, meditation, ritual, bathing, socializing or game playing for every one of work. For all that the modern period has sought to embarrass the past by stressing lack of comfort and excessive, grubby toil, the year 1000 involved considerably less effort, expenditure and waste of energy than the year 2000.

The Black Death of 1347–52 cropped the population of Europe by upwards of a third, encouraging a workforce to move away from land and loyalty to money and mobility. But it was the Protestant Reformation that installed a culture of work through religious doctrine, with Calvinism providing, in the words of social historian Barbara Ehrenreich, 'a transcendent rationale for this shift, intensifying isolation and practically institutionalizing depression as a stage in the quest for salvation'. It was no longer enough to pray to St. Teresa, celebrate Jesus through dance or chant at your local well. Surviving pagan and Celtic Christian aspects of the church were replaced with an increasingly Puritan ethic that made salvation possible only through continual hard work. Former sacred acts like dancing and games were demonized and only work resulting in financial reward was encouraged. According to Ehrenreich, festivities were 'just another bad habit the lower classes would have to be weaned from, like the English workers' observance of "St. Monday" as a day to continue, or recuperate from, the weekend's fun'. The arrival of the gun in the 1600s as the weapon of choice, with its complex method of assembling, arming, firing, cleaning and reloading, turned combat into a lifestyle; drilling the new army proletariat into automata who were forbidden time to idle. Guns ground down the individual soldier to the level of a cog in a giant war machine and Oliver Cromwell's New Model Army was a prime example of this method and a taste of what was to come. Hard work was equated with military, financial and spiritual success, while indolence meant damnation.

It was with this maniac work ethic that Empire developed and this Little Britain became *Great*. The ability to create steam and power engines transformed the speed with which raw materials could be transported, colonial produce shipped and the landscape drastically disfigured. The agrarian and industrial revolutions made physical alterations of the environment possible on a scale never before witnessed. It meant money and power for those who owned the land and technology, and it offered the most dramatic incentive to a workforce who fled the closed (and now enclosed) parishes for the bright lights of furnace and factory. Technology, housing and transportation all marked the city out from the country. And like Dick Whittington, people expected to find the streets paved with gold. There was definitely money to be made diving into the seething sprawl of industry, but at what cost?

It was many decades after the mass project of urban and industrial building that the issues of social welfare, sanitation and health were finally acknowledged. Towns like Merthyr Tydfil in South Wales were summoned up like genii to house a growing workforce that labored from as soon as they were able until they dropped. Once everything useful had been stripped from the Earth, such towns, and their redundant labor markets, were left to rot, useless in the face of a new global empire that was repeating the process of smash and grab in other, cheaper, lands. Less tangible, the balance of life between action and rest, doing and being, was scuppered. Like the Puritan theology and army discipline, the rising factories demanded unending work. The dominance of money as the symbol of exchange meant those committed to the march of progress couldn't afford to be left behind.

In booming cities like London, New York and Tokyo, electricity replaced coal and gas, and the determination to build more, move faster and climb higher accelerated. Across the western world we are still laboring, in shops and offices rather than mills and mines, irrespective of hour of day or season, fearful of sickness impeding us, impatient if the computerized systems don't respond immediately, running up debts to buy the gadgets and improvements sold to us as consolation for the lack of time and space we find hemming us in. Like the treadmills of so many fitness centers, we only know that we must run further, faster and harder. If we risk stopping, the machine will hurl us to the floor. And while air travel and the Internet mean we can connect with the whole world in an instant, the speed leaves us incapable of those qualities of relish, absorption and relaxation that give meaning to life and require time more than money.

The industrial machine has proved successful beyond the capability of the Earth to support it and our individual capacities working at this pace seem equally fraught. Our heads ache, our bodies suffer, our fast cars frustrate us on congested roads. Yet the principles of hard work remain, almost hard-wired into us: that it's a good thing, that we are achieving our goals and advancing. Onward Christian soldiers! But as the oil reserves that fuel our appetite for speed dwindle and the environmental and human costs of operating at such artificially fast levels grow, the question needs asking: to where exactly are we racing?

The difference between the masculine and feminine ways of

being can be applied to time. Under his-story, time has been repeatedly written as the straight line of the masculine digit (1): as linear time; from A to B; measured like the divisions on a yardstick. In the beginning was the word and it ends in revelation. Linear time makes sense of measurement and accomplishment: competing to be first past the post or scoring the most goals in 90 minutes. According to linear time running faster makes sense. Under linear time, George Stephenson's rocket makes sense. Under linear time, Jeremy Clarkson makes sense.

But linear time is only half the story. There is also circular time, the rotation of spheres, changes in seasons, the rise and fall and rise of the breath. The spiral that moves by returning to the start point again: same, same but different. Circular time can be seen on every round clock face with the movement of hands back to the position at which they start. The importance of circular time appears again and again from those indigenous cultures that were assimilated by the vast march of his-story. Literary theorist Eva Knudsen writes, 'The traditional Maori conception of development as a form of spiraling progression ... is seen to carry, intrinsically, the seeds of its own continuing renewal.' Within Native American experience, the circle turns back and turns in on itself: completing and renewing. Such circularities do not limit or separate our existence into start and finish. They are constantly rotating, unfolding and folding back, allowing for growth and transformation. As writer Jill Purce says, 'Time itself is cyclic, and by the spiral of its returning seasons we review the progress and growth of our own understanding.' The cycle is infinite and endless, so relax yourself!

In cultures where circular time is given as much attention as linear time, people's lives are far more relaxed and stress-free. Most traditional aboriginal people work far fewer hours, at most two or three days out of each week. And this is not *working* as we understand it; they visit, hang out, talk and gossip, ensuring that the social cement that holds their society together is in good order. To live with circular time is to let go of deadlines. Circular time encourages meditation, idling, play. It is often one of the biggest surprises for people who take their foot off the pedal, to find a richer, simpler and more rewarding life. Their bodies are rested, they enjoy better health and they smile more. More often they create and play and remember what it was like to be a child, where the journey from A to B was seldom straight and never narrow. Their ability to access subtle details increases. They breathe in the world.

What is the point of striving, adversely affecting your being and that of your environment to end up at exactly the same place? It's like the tale of the woman who lived on a beach, with a small hut, a warm fire and a wide view. One day she was sitting on her favorite chair, enjoying some salt fish and watching the sun sink into the sea. She heard the fast pad of exhausted footsteps on the sand, way before the sunburnt man strode up to her.

'That fish smells good,' said the man.

'Have some,' the woman offered with a smile. 'I caught it fresh today.'

The man took a bite. 'Incredible! You know,' he continued, talking while he ate, 'if you were to spend more of your day fishing you could have enough fish to take to the market to sell.'

'Indeed,' said the woman. 'Why would I do that?'

'Ah well,' said the man, 'if you sold your fish at market you could make money. Then you could buy a bigger boat, you could go further from this bay and collect more fish. You would then be able to pay other people to fish for you.'

'And why would I want to do that?' asked the woman again.

'With people working for you, you could expand, sell more fish, get more money, buy more boats and establish a factory. You could can the fish and sell it further away, overseas even. You could sell shares, become a company; you're guaranteed to make great profits.'

'Wow. That sounds a mighty lot of work,' the woman said, shaking her head. 'Tell me why I'd want to do that?'

The man looked pleased with himself. 'Because once you get rich, you could retire and do absolutely nothing but find a quiet beach somewhere, watch the sunset and eat a piece of fish.'

Settling into Cells

The world is in chaos. In the mid 20th century Benoit Mandelbrot developed his mathematics of fractals and chaos theory, which helped show, from smoke and clouds to cliffs and ferns, the shapes of our world growing in imperfectly symmetric patterns of self-similarity. But for thousands of years mathematics has boxed up the weird and spiraling into fixed forms with different angles and numbers of sides, collaborating to produce shapes familiar to any geometry class. For all the fuzz, blob and serpent of nature, oblongs and squares are the blocks we've used to build over her.

The idea to build in stone came around 5,000 years ago from the need of the new, masculine way of thinking to mark the meeting of humanity with the divinity he had just separated. Julian Cope says, in the introduction to his comprehensive megalithic gazetteer of the UK, *The Modern Antiquarian,*

> The majority of Britain's stone circles, dolmens and chambered Cairns are close to 5000 years old and they are examples of the very first monuments ever built by Humankind. Before that time we had felt no need for monuments, for the earth was our home and Humanity did not consider itself in any way separate ... We worshipped at great waterfalls, sacred trees, or at natural rocky outcrops of significance. But the coming of agriculture brought with it a certain degree of independence and control over the land.

As soon as man moved a stone to distinguish 'this' from 'that', the separation began. It's comparable with the separation of the growing ego of a child as they pass from feeling connected with everything. Jill Purce notes,

> In the early days of humanity, as in childhood, there was no separation between ourselves and the outside world, until we, individually or as a race, became self-conscious. Once the ego crystallized and we saw ourselves as subject and distinct from the world, the continuum differentiated into things. Each branched into more things, which in turn branched into even more, until the continuum had developed into a hierarchy.

One of the earliest loci of this separation was between the chaotic waters and the dry land. To honor the human understanding of a separate experience on land, the mountain was revered. Many of the earliest and most impressive examples of building work (Giza, Chichen Itza and Angkor Wat) reflect a pyramidal shape in honor of the mountain. The marriage of heaven and earth, of the swirling waters below and the land above, might also explain the wider practice in antiquity of siting sacred buildings immediately above underground springs and watercourses. Maybe this was an attempt to honor both sides of the divide. After all, the body of the temple was intended to express the union of humanity and divinity.

Even our most treasured ancient megaliths, like those at Stonehenge, are testimony to this segregation, though the recurrence of circles and the placing of stones at perceived energy points along the leys of the land imply an understanding of a whole greater than the sum of the separated parts.

While his-story built first with the intention of honoring the relationship between the newly divorced worlds, it was men who were doing the measuring. The separation of sacred from profane moved us away from the divine feminine that makes everything whole. As his-story unfolded, the enduring shape of built-things settled into the square form. Architecture moved from the Temple to the kind of materialism that thousands of years later would litter the hills with flat pack retail parks. In part this was because of the other partnering concerns of his-story. The association between agriculture and cities in the hands of hierarchical bands of armed men meant it would not be long before building came to demonstrate, not spiritual importance, but the material wealth of the richest landowners. And whether for god or shipping magnate, the shape of all this building work was excessively square. When divine proportion went out of the square window, buildings went up according to fashion, until anything went, as long as it stood up. Whether to house power stations or art works, these buildings were almost universally four-sided.

If buildings represent how we make sense of the world then a lot of our contemporary struggles have deep roots in what the unbalanced legacy of this age did to our need for shelter. For one thing, a square building discourages flow. Things smack against hard edges and get trapped in tight spots; our backs get put up against the wall. Square buildings partition life into my room/your room: upstairs/downstairs: our side of the fence and the wrong side of the tracks. Developing a sense of four-walled living reaffirms division.

Few of us know how different it feels to be in a circular space, but those building low-impact roundhouses out of wood and cob, erecting tipis and gers, are shaping living arrangements which will help all of us remember harmony and belonging. There is no sudden break in the wall. Life flows freely and circulates according to the feminine principle. People sit in circle, rather than on one side of the room or another. Looking up at the roof at night reminds us of the natural world we're part of, the circle of sky and revolving constellations. There is peace rather than a disjoining quarrel of right angles. (One might ask: what would make a *wrong* angle?) And groups of roundhouses tend towards forming larger circles, like the arrangement of prehistoric roundhouses at the restored camp of Castell Henllys in West Wales. Living in circles brings us together, reminds us of what we have in common and what connects us. In circle we are all equidistant from the center, with the children sitting closest to the fire. Circles help us reaffirm tribal bonds and focus energy on those missing due to sickness.

By building at right angles we have moved far from the spirit level of the Earth. We have forgotten that life can be simple and joyous and enough. The further we have gone, the less satisfied and at home we feel, hence the more complex structures we've believed to be necessary. It is not a development that everyone has rushed to embrace, as Sitting Bull observed to his people when the white settlers advanced across America in the 1800s:

> You hear me, my people, we now have to deal with another race … Strangely enough they have a mind to till the soil and the love of possessions is a disease with them … they claim this mother of ours, this earth, for their own, fence their neighbors away; they deface her with their buildings and their refuse.

By fencing ourselves off, children and adults have deserted each other; tribes have vanished, the extended family has turned nuclear until the many boxes that were sold as proof of definition against your neighbors expanded across the land to cope with both the exploding population and the atomization of families. These distinctions have multiplied across studios and one-bedroom apartments, as the boxes became further divided to meet the minimum requirements of single-cell existence. We have fractured to the furthest possible extent, and the only thing that brings us together now is the square screen of television and computer keeping us in touch. Virtually.

The buildings we live in, fostering segregation over unity, have shaped our sense of isolation and engendered fear. One of the few circular buildings ever designed in the west was a prison: Jeremy Bentham's Panopticon. Bentham's vision was of a stately pleasure dome comparable to the Circus at Bath. An ideal prison, it used the circular principle of inclusion to set up a surveillance system where every prisoner would be under total scrutiny. In John Twelve Hawks' near-future fantasy *The Traveler*, the Panopticon is the name given to the chain of CCTV cameras recording everything. And while the circle offers no corners in which to hide, to use it as a means of punishment, restraint and paranoia says a lot about how this age has viewed the concept of togetherness.

To be excluded from the circle was the ultimate punishment in tribal societies. For a worldview based on relationships, the threat of banishment is far more serious than life imprisonment or the death penalty. It means cutting people off from the whole society and from the opportunity to hear and speak their own language. It removes the very context that gives a person's life meaning and identity. His-story has found other rules and methods of imprisonment. Rather than feel banished from their community, prisoners find themselves welcomed into the new community of prison: in gated groups of cells, not so unlike those masquerading as the height of city chic. What's so bad about being sent to dwell in square rooms, with beds, toilets and televisions, separated by walls from your neighbors (whom you only see when you venture out to get food) and estranged from Nature? It's home from home. And even the restrictions of being locked up against your will and serving a sentence with little option of leaving are not so different from many people's experience of the urban snare; tied into mortgage contracts and a 40-hour working week to honor them. After all, the purpose of prison, as French philosopher Jean Baudrillard says, is 'to hide that it is the social in its entirety, in its banal omnipresence, that is carceral'.

It was modernist architects of the 20th century, led by figures like Le Corbusier, Mies Van De Roy and designers at the Bauhaus, who realized the shape of things to come. They understood that an exponentially increasing human population would need to be housed, so they designed huge tower blocks of identical rooms in cell-like combination. Mass buildings were needed to store the large batteries of humanity, whether in education, hospitals, prisons, offices or homes. When the economy recovered after the Second World War, cities across this island would become breezy with blocks of such rooms piled high.

Contemporary structures offer a sense of interchangeability. Any square room seems to do. So people live in former warehouses and schools and create office spaces in spare rooms. Even a Victorian prison, like the one at Oxford, is effortlessly converted into luxury hotel accommodation. But to see our domestic space as no different from where we work or face imprisonment is to wonder what, in settling down, we have brought upon ourselves. It might seem a vast leap to link agriculture with modern isolation, with its keys, entry codes and constant surveillance, but the root of our modern settlements lies in the organization of land according to agricultural principles of division and ownership. As soon as we fenced off the first square of land to imprison animals, we did the same to ourselves. Mass farming and battery chickens should disturb us, not just for the prisons we make for our animals, but for the unflinching mirror they hold up to how we have imprisoned ourselves.

Finding our way out of these cells requires a power greater than the individual. To come together and find a way back into harmony with our Earth; to have the confidence and ability to throw away the bundles of keys that separate us; to respect that we are all tenants of this life, who don't own our bodies and who borrow the land from our children; to enjoy the free availability of everything that grows, with the responsibility of understanding how our actions impact on us – this will be our challenge and our reward. While our cells are padded with comfort and our screens entertain us and whatever the state of the land, our shelves are full of food, it might seem a challenge not worth engaging with. It depends on how important this freedom is for us. It also depends on how much longer we will be able to continue living this model, before the consequences break in on us with more weight than all the burglars we hoped would stay banged up.

Animal Crackers

The fridge magnet reads: 'Cats were once worshipped as Gods. Cats have never forgotten this.' Ancient Egypt recognized the potency of animals and afforded them the status of divinity. Indigenous American tribes carved features of power animals in the form of totem poles, recognizing the wisdom and talents of these life forms. Aboriginal creation myths within The Dreaming talk of ancestors singing everything into creation, with each animal and tribe being born by its totem (animal) parent. Within the islands of Britain a form of totemism existed among the Celts, with tribes, groups and individuals adopting an animal whose characteristics they admired and felt an association with. But within the loaded polarities of his-story animals have been reduced to the opposite of how the defining men have seen themselves. Man was intelligent, reasonable and superior. Animals were dumb, beastly and filthy. Thanks to the prevailing ideology, we no longer have respect for animals. We have battery farms, pet shops and insecticides.

Our fellow animals are just one of the many forms of life to have come off badly under this last age. Incapable of speaking in the languages of humanity, they have been ridiculed and ignored. Their sounds have been mimicked, the meaning of their songs and their power lost. We stopped listening to them and rendered them mute. But if they could speak in our tongue their experiences of this age might sound like the dolphins in Carol Ann Duffy's poem of the same title:

> We are in our element but we are not free ... We sink
> to the limits of this pool until the whistle blows.
> There is a man and our mind knows we will die here.

The justification for this control is embedded in the beginning of his-story with the male god of Genesis giving man dominion over all animals. No longer respected as different but equal, they are hence subordinated and stratified depending on their usefulness: the saddled horse, the obedient dog and the stupid cow. As with so much indigenous wisdom, the role of sacred animals faded under ecclesiastical pressure to view them as walking dinner with no special attributes. The honoring of a totem animal often involved treating it as kin, listening to it, observing it, feeling it. It was prohibited to kill one's own totem animal, although it could be consumed on one special day each year. Dressing in a totem animal's skin was done to better imagine, identify with and act out their attributes and habits. But the trend of this age persistently forbade such relationships. In 669 AD a papal dispensation was issued ordering, 'Whoever at the kalends [1st] of January goes about in the form of a stag, that is changing himself into the form of an animal ... penance for three years, because it is devilish.' In the aligning of the world according to *good* or *bad*, animals were compartmentalized with Satan. It is no coincidence that the enduring icon for the devil, with horns, hooves and a tail, contains so many animal attributes.

The idea of human/animal transformation is central to shamanic practice and is suggested in many of the cave paintings of our ancestors from 30,000 years ago. The world's three oldest collections of figurative art all prominently feature fabulous creatures that are part beast and part human. There is evidence of transformation throughout Greek mythology, with, amongst others, Zeus turning into a swan and Arachne being transfigured into a spider. Within Celtic mythology, too, characters transform themselves into animals by metamorphosis. Taliesin, perhaps the most powerful shamanic figure in Welsh folklore, turned into a hare, a fish and a bird, in his attempts to flee Ceridwen's wrath. But even in terms of simply communicating with animals we appear to have lost the knack. In Native America, elders tell stories of a time when humans and animals could freely talk together. Before the coming of this age, who knows how extensive that communication between all aspects of Nature may have been?

But the demonization of animals through this age has resulted in a collective panic, where anything that squawks, roars or splashes is considered better caged. I went to London Zoo recently, having never been before. It was a sobering experience. Hordes of humans stepped up to glass fronts and bars making faces, safe in the learned knowledge of dominance; peering at the creatures on the other side with a mix of repulsion, mockery and superiority. Of the animals themselves, a sense of damage and depression pervaded. Fish made endless loops within the squeeze of a tank; big cats, sunk in lethargy hid as far from the cawing visitors as they could; apes and monkeys held their heads in their hands. This was their life; trapped and put on show for people to point at.

Separate from Nature, we like our natural world to jump at our demands like dolphins through hoops. As self-proclaimed masters of the world we do not need to risk ourselves in it, especially when animals can be tranquilized, transported and set to live out their days in the confines of an exhibit. It gives the paying public a chance to study animals they wouldn't otherwise see, so the logic goes. Which is to say, they get to see animals imprisoned and stripped of their dignity. Of course, when you have a one-sided system of kings, with assumed divine power over all people, then animals become just another equation of wealth and dominance; all life in unopposed service to man. And the trickle-down effect is that people subordinated within the system take the chance to get supremacy over those beneath them - like the cleaner who repeatedly beat and stabbed Annie the circus elephant in 2011. The bullied find solace in acting out the bully elsewhere.

The rise of science took the objectification of other life a step further. Man now had the *right* not just to own animals, but to kill and dissect them; sending back specimens to be labeled, compartmentalized and pickled; useful to theories of evolution and to the dominance of scientific objectivity that believed it could contain and explain everything. They began to be bred in laboratories, fed and tested with drugs for the beautification and betterment of people. They have been sent into space, tagged and placed in captivity, with no say in the matter.

The *right* of humans to eat meat has veered away from the sacred practice of hunting, which once drew humans and animals together in a co-operative movement and a complex dance of time and season. Now technology enables us to kill for one meager part (as with sharks, which are caught, have their fins sliced off, and then are thrown back into the seas to drown) or for human fun (pheasants are bred simply for the sport of being released and shot, more often left to rot than eaten). Our taste for flesh as nothing more than something to be filleted for the choicest cuts has encouraged deforestation and meaningless, vacuous slaughter.

To evolutionists like Richard Dawkins, all life is 'an arms race', a battle between kill or be killed, with only the fittest surviving long enough to breed. But even if we take the existence of all life as one giant scramble to live long enough to make babies, it is still much more than this *either/or* paradigm. It is kill and be killed. Every animal has to eat to survive and even our jungle kings are not immune to death, serving up their carcasses to scavengers, insects and worms. To see animals as locked in some bitter fight to the death is nothing more than to project our own limited vision of a battle-crazed world onto them.

While we crack the circus whip to make big cats obedient, it is the smallest animals that exert a perpetual nuisance. We find our Nemesis in those creatures that move too swiftly to be captured, breed so prolifically and adapt too rapidly to the best insecticides technology can supply. The fallacy of all pesticides is, as Rachel Carson observed in her seminal environmental work *Silent Spring*, that, 'New insect generations arise in a matter of days or weeks.' Our need to farm more intensively struggles against the appetites of insects, and our fear of them as disease-bringers highlights our own insecurity in the 'dog eat dog' tale we've spun. Because while showstoppers like lions and sharks make us quake, it is the smallest of animals – the insects, worms, parasites and bacteria – that really bug us. They, more than any other animal, are pervasive, ancient and continually haunt us by threatening to do to us what we insist is our *right* to do to the rest of life. They decimate us. They feast on our blood, infect us with viruses, and even if we reach the end of our lives unplagued by them, our buried corpses become their banquet. The evolutionists' panic of 'kill or be killed' sets us in a feverish race with all other life; we have to be masters or we're not playing the game. The irony is that in trying to flee from these little mites we are creating poisons more deadly to our survival than a swamp of malarial mosquitoes.

In shaping the world as one of dire survival at all costs, we risk forgetting what animals intuitively understand: that it's a game to be enjoyed. We all have the same destination, whether manta ray or investment banker. And like the adage I heard when learning to surf, 'The best surfer is the one having the most fun.' Much as the fear of theft is dependent on the principle of private property, our separation from Nature has increased our sense of its threat. In philosophical terms, it is akin to the cheerless theories of Thomas Hobbes, who said we live in continual danger and hence must stab the stranger who approaches us before they have a chance to stab us. It is not only dull to reduce all the experiences of life to the most functional rites. According to the biologist Elaine Morgan it is suicidal:

> The scientific zeitgeist says we have four basic urges, the four 'F's: feeding, fleeing, fighting and fucking. And as long as we

> can do these, everything else comes second. I say if you had a race that had only those, they would be extinct within a generation. You have to have fostering, feeling for others, family and fun. But because these qualities don't fit into their scheme, the scientific establishment argues as if they're not there. That's a very male attitude.

Among those who take the time to observe animals, there is the awareness that a vast amount of play is undertaken. This celebration of life for no other purpose than life itself seems to have the same appeal as play has for us. It's fun. It makes us happy. Play among animals occurs, in the words of Richard Mabey, 'throughout the natural world, in displays which clearly show a relishing of sensual experience and interaction with other creatures (and sometimes other species)'. Dolphins surf waves, gulls glide on thermals, and starlings perform spectacular crepuscular dances, until 'at times it seems as if the whole company of nature, ourselves included, is simply at play'. It is of course possible to flatten every activity to the grimly functional, but what does the determination to reduce the richness, variety and enjoyment of the world to this fraught battleground say about us? Is the idea that Nature needs taming meant to justify our own regimes and scare us away from it; painting it as a dangerous jungle of potential killers to keep us domiciled? If it is, then locked in our hermetic households we are in real danger of suffocating. Our ability to prevent infection rests on the health of our immune system, which play supports because it makes us feel safe, relaxed and happy.

The indigenous peoples of the Americas are an example of a people whose cosmological ideas of the world were so encompassing and inclusive that western diseases decimated them. It was akin to boatloads of cell phone salesmen arriving in a primary school. It is generally assumed that the first diseases to enter the New World were brought by human contact, but there is the additional suggestion of cross-species contamination. A great epidemic of many diseases may have begun in the animal population and spread westward from the coast. The potency of diseases within animals to affect humans was greater because, unlike in the Old World, the two-legged and the four-legged had maintained a harmonious relationship. Having understood the symbiosis of Nature, and honored it, they were now becoming locked together in a terrible symbiosis of disease. A wave of sickness, affecting humans and animals alike, radiated in advance of the first missionaries and explorers. Are we yet ready to see the mindsets we've encouraged over this period as not merely destructive to our land and animals but, because of the interrelation of all things, perniciously destructive to ourselves?

Then we have the other side of our schizophrenic attitude to the natural world: the recognition that some animals are worthy of our affections. Cats and dogs are the favorites. Here they are, the acceptable face of the animal world, those we can fuss over. Rather than see all life as sacred and worthy of respect (whether it be jaguar, bear or spider), we have decided some are *good* and some are *bad*: the white mice, helpful in the laboratory, *versus* the black, plague-spreading rat. The prioritized ones get the prize of being able to live almost like us. We buy them processed meat from the supermarket, take them to be injected and dress them in Burberry, the lucky dogs!

Yet we are so distorted in our vision of life that we treat even these animals as nothing more than living toys which we gift at Christmas, then abuse so abysmally they are thrown out of cars in sacks. Some of the dogs rescued by animal sanctuaries, such as The Dogs' Trust, are so traumatized by the fickleness of humanity they can never again be housed with people. It seems that even with animals we deem worthy we are not consistent; smothering, rejecting, chastising and dismissing them when we are bored; unleashing our own terrible impotencies onto them. Much ill treatment of pets, especially dogs, comes from regarding them as child substitutes or status symbols. Britain may consider itself to be a nation of animal lovers, but the record of domestic animal abuse, let alone intensive farming and blood sports, suggests anything but.

For all we crimp our poodles and dress up our cats, we are no closer to respecting the natural world and the inhabitants we share it with. If we dare to remember that a divine spiritual energy flows through every life form, this behavior is shocking. So long as we are content to believe in a purely material world, with the rights of man separate from and superior over the rights of all other life, then we have the ideology to abuse, farm and slaughter at our leisure. But we should not be surprised when Nature responds. As Alice Walker writes of her meeting with a horse, Blue, 'Most disturbing of all, in Blue's large brown eyes was a new look, more painful than the look of despair: the look of disgust with human beings, with life; the look of hatred.' If the alienation of all other life is proof of our victory in the battle for survival, what does that make this survival worth?

Scientists might not be willing to afford all life a living spirit, but they do at least grant some life consciousness, which they then rate according to a number of tests, ranging from those which qualify as human by being able to recognize their image in a mirror, downwards. Richard Mabey observes becoming 'oddly attracted to the idea of vegetativeness, of trying to tune in with other kinds of mind that operate on the earth without the privilege of self-consciousness ... to work at gently joining our ancient, shared sense more closely with our actions'. Even by the hierarchical definitions of science, there are profoundly intelligent animals killed by sub-aquatic sonic assaults from military tests, whose habitats are destroyed without consideration, whose purpose is reduced to being poked and pointed at in cages. To treat the rest of life as we do, reducing its potential, delineating good from bad, intensively breeding what we like and no less intensively exterminating what we don't, claiming to love, while not yet seeming sure how to respect, once again we provide nothing more than the living example of how we are treating ourselves.

Color Me Bad

Color is one of the gifts we have in this world. Within the spectrum there are different hues and all of these colors have associations. Some people dig the blues. Others plump not for lapis or turquoise but cerulean. Which colors are good? Is pink bad? Are some yellows better than others?

It is even harder to take our cultural obsession with morality seriously when it is applied to color, yet within his-story that's exactly what has happened. Admittedly, the range was more limited. I can't think off-hand of any wars fought against tangerine. But color bias has had a far more serious and long-lasting legacy, in the form of the division between black and white. As the standard bearers of monotheism moved further north, so color and its absence became the basis for extreme patterns of thought and behavior. The white dove became a symbol of peace, and black cats faced mass extermination because the color of their coats was supposed to make them associates of the devil.

And the prime victims of this polarized vision of the world were the people whose skin color was named 'black' by the law-giving whites. The ludicrous idea of turning the colorful world monochrome and assigning virtues and vices to each half had the effect of vilifying Nature, women and those whose skin color was dark. In the words of Luce Irigaray, 'Forcing races, traditions, sexes and generations to conform to a single model of identity, culture and civilisation means subjecting them to an order which does not take into account their differences.' That the colonizers who reached the shores of Africa, like the Holy Crusaders who reached Jerusalem, were marching with a code for such division in the form of their bible, made the insanity appear god-given. Race philosopher Frantz Fanon paraphrases their logic: 'The good and merciful God cannot be black: He is a white man with bright pink cheeks.' Rather than arrive in another part of the world and seek to learn from the inhabitants' wisdom and culture, white colonists arrived to tell them how their skin color made them savage and how they would be bettered by the arriving pale skins, who were angelic and as pure as god. These newcomers said (in the words of Fanon), 'We are the chosen people – look at the color of our skins. The others are black or yellow: That is because of their sins.' In the idea of race, it was the white men who set the agenda and claimed supremacy.

And it was this same philosophy that was behind the refining process – now named as one of the ills of the modern diet. Sugar, flour, rice and paper have all witnessed the polarity that white is *good* and black (or brown, natural or wild) is *bad*. As an innately brown substance, sugar couldn't be countenanced on the tables of those Europeans who considered white as the height of social achievement. People, as well as commodities, were assessed in terms of their rudeness or refinement. To counter the risk of being thought rude, it was deemed preferable to develop bleaching and whitening processes, carried out in factories to remove impurities, for all the belching chimneys erected among the poorer districts that blackened the workers' homes and lives. Even in 2008 the power of bleaching seemed intact when a celebrated African-American singer like Beyoncé appeared several tones lighter in her L'Oréal adverts, and when the brown-skinned doll Upsy Daisy (from the UK children's TV series *In the Night Garden*) was manufactured to appear white.

The morality of color is rooted within our culture, with black equaling *evil*. Fear of what was natural alienated people from the land, with all its brown mud and dirt. To the dominant ideology, the savage, like Nature, was wild and had to be tamed. It helped the expansion of slavery and justified the use of torture, rape, mutilation and mass deportation. When Columbus found the Indies in 1492, it was in the aftermath of Spain's internal wars against Jews and Muslims. And though, as historian Dr. Eric

Williams argues, the reason for slavery was economic as much as moral, it can't be ignored that 'racial difference made it easier to justify and rationalize Negro slavery, to exact the mechanical obedience of a plough-ox or cart-horse, to demand that complete moral and intellectual subjugation'.

Slavery was not first developed by colonizing Europeans but went back to the birth of his-story, when the division of the world made some people into slaves; dismissing them as beasts of burden with human faces. It had thousands of years to become an acceptable aspect of Greek and Roman societies and among those very masculinized African tribes who were to find themselves on the other end of the chain once the Europeans came. Chinua Achebe's novel *Things Fall Apart* shows the effect of the accompanying partner to economic servitude, religious subservience, under the crusading missionaries: 'Mr. Brown's successor was the Reverend James Smith … He saw things as black and white. And black was evil.' But the male-dominated Nigerian tribes he was civilizing already knew and worshipped *mastery*, having already made a slave of the feminine. The 'tall and huge' hero of Achebe's story, Okonkwo, fearing the ultimate shame of being associated with woman, told them 'masculine stories of violence and bloodshed'. The irony of the enslaved being as capable themselves of slavery is explored in Grace Nichols' poem 'Taint', where she writes,

> But I was traded by men
> the color of my own skin …
> No it isn't easy to forget
> what we refuse to remember.

Yet whatever slavery had taken place within West African society was nothing compared to the huge enterprise of European-driven slavery that saw between 11 and 20 million black men, women and children, exported in chains and coffins across the

Atlantic to the sugar, tobacco and cotton plantations of the New World; hurling themselves into the sea or being crudely ejected when sick. It is ironic that an article as sweet as sugar should have occasioned such bloodshed. To those, like poet Merle Collins, who return to the suffering of their ancestors, they find cave dungeons,

> packed with bodies, where bones were left
> where uncovered graves were made, where whispers echo still.

Slavery was another instance in the 5,000-year-old epoch of his-story where an idea of division was leant credence by the greed of the few who stood to make themselves materially rich from its implementation.

There are people who still believe in a religious or scientific justification for discrimination on the basis of color. Still the code of division and supremacy survives to encourage modern fascist parties like the British National Party and English Defence League in their nationalistic racism. The concept of 'Institutional Racism', as voiced by Black Power activists Stokely Carmichael and Charles Hamilton in America in the 1960s, that 'all whites benefitted from social structures and organizational patterns which continually disadvantaged blacks', still has too much currency. In the UK, children like Stephen Lawrence and Damilola Taylor are still murdered because of the color of their skin, which is (as the report on the murder of Ahmed Iqbal Ullah in 1986 concludes) 'an outcome of the generalized culture of masculinized violence in schools'. The dichotomy between the good whites at war with the evil blacks is so ingrained that, for some, the American 'War on Terror' with the Islamic world needs little extrapolation. And a report by Clearcast revealed that, despite comprising around 13% of the population of the UK, black, Asian and other ethnic minority groups appeared in only

5% of 35,000 TV adverts screened in 2010

But this time of transition is inviting the voicing and hearing of different stories. It is only now, 200 years after the abolition of slavery in the UK, that experiences belonging to the ones who were ill-treated are being heard and apologies issued. In 2008 for the first time, the History of Slavery became mandatory in the GCSE History exam syllabus. The returning narratives to balance the long-dominant one come like thundering rivers undamning themselves: as in Maya Angelou's poem 'Africa':

Now she is rising
remember her pain
remember her losses
her screams loud and vain
remember her riches
her history slain
Now she is striding
Although she had lain.

'Love see no color', or rather, see the spectrum in which we all figure. Because as easy as it is to reduce the world to black or white, the truth is billions of pigmentations, including a range of tones from salmon, almond and peach through to mahogany, ebony and clay. As a saying that someone forwarded in an email has it: 'You go red when you're embarrassed, purple when you're angry, yellow when you're sick, green when you're jealous, blue when you're cold ... And you have the cheek to call *us* colored.' And as the cultures become ever more mixed, as different tribes and races combine, so more generations are born enriching the mix and confusing the arbitrary boundaries further.

We are blessed with color in this world. Blessed to have sunsets and blossom, glaciers and midnight. The harmonies and contrasts wear their varying coats with the effortless confidence of knowing they only add to the world. And if a color is reappearing at this time of transition, it is plural. The word 'rainbow' signifies diversity, especially of racial and cultural minorities. The rainbow flag is hoisted up to signify peace, to celebrate diversity in sex, gender and sexuality and to remind us of our sacred pledge to honor and protect our environment, of which we are all a part. Being green might be akin to the experience that the explorer Bruce Parry had, having taken the plant Iboga when staying with the Babongo tribe in the Congo:

> I saw a swathe of green mist passing between us. It left my chest and passed to M. Hugue's chest and then onto Jean Claude's and all round the circle of Buriti papas … This mist joined us to the forest and all the animals and plants within it. We were all just tiny parts of our huge breathing organism of a planet.

The rainbow spectrum honors diversity of humanity, biodiversity in the natural world; is harmonized in the chakra wheels of increased consciousness, and promotes greater spiritual understanding and inclusion. The rainbow arches over all of us, visible arc of a bigger circle that brings us together in our differences. No evil color exists and nor does any right one. Just color, simple, elusive, identifiable and ephemeral.

Consider the world's diversity and worship it. Like the world, color is everywhere in variation: some cool, some hot, others dazzling. There may be one idea of purple, but in that slim band is an infinity of variants. God, like color, exists in every living thing, every rock and star and relationship. But, like color, she can only be witnessed in the plural. She is everywhere, and every shade of science and poetry and myth makes a song of her. His-story might have made enemies of the white and black notes, but music needs both. Fundamentalism might, out of fear, feel the need to reduce the world to monochrome, but as children, and everyone who has watched *The Wizard of Oz*, knows: life sings better in color.

Body and Soul

What do you get if you repeatedly tell a story that punishes one sex and its attributes and elevates the other to godly status? Of course: it's a joke.

The body has become the most personal battleground of his-story. According to this age's propensity to divide and categorize, woman became associated with 'the body' to man's thinking. To the reasoning of the dominant masculine ideology, the natural body, with its morass of sticky desire and messy substances, was looked down upon. In 423 AD Simeon Stylites the Elder climbed up a pillar in Syria and remained there until his death 37 years later, so desperate was he to literally raise himself above the sweat and feast of bodily function.

In light of the fear with which his-story viewed the body, the act of sex needed to be cautioned against, blocked and restricted. Chastity, the withholding of sexual energy, was interpreted as a badge of victory: the masculine 'mind' triumphant over the feminine 'body'. Purity became associated with self-denial. Again and again during this age, sexuality was imagined as a danger zone; a mire of irrational forces leading to depravity, lust and ultimately hell. In the words of Simone de Beauvoir, 'Original sin makes of the body the enemy of the soul ... all ties of the flesh seem evil.'

Jesus' conception hits upon this vexing question of sex. Rather than be sullied by conception, Jesus' mother Mary is able to conceive without soiling herself. This example of virgin birth was not unique prior to the coming of monotheism. The Melissae, within the tradition of the Path of Pollen, and virgin priestess-hoods in antiquity, sought to emulate the example of the Queen bee, which was parthenogenic and divinely able to give birth to an egg without it being fertilized. The biblical Mary may have been a priestess dedicated to virgin birth, specifically as an elevated form of spiritual practice. But in the organization of Jesus' story by the church fathers, the Immaculate Conception removed power from the female (Mary's own working of her internal sacred laboratory) and handed it to the male God who enabled her. In the words of 'radical and revolting hag' Mary Daly, the story is 'the opposite of parthenogenesis, for in the myth of the Virgin Birth, Mary does nothing, whereas in parthenogenesis the female accomplishes everything herself'. Mary is enshrined within the Catholic faith as the highest form of woman, and becomes an impossible example to follow. She erases the potential of other women to procreate without a man, by handing the task to a god who won't repeat it.

On the opposite side sits the other Mary: Magdalene. The woman condemned for loving sex was arguably closer to Jesus during his own lifetime than any other. This example of woman, embodied and emboldened, accessing her sexual power without guilt or angst, becomes another Eve; a villainess, a warning of the dangers of sex, tempting the would-be-sexless masculine head towards animalistic urges and base desires. While Mary the Virgin becomes a powerful idol of the so-called *ideal*, Mary Magdalene becomes a leper and her sacred images are defaced. There is fire and fury at her being, and any suggestion she might have slept with Jesus, even carried his child and carried on the bloodline (Holy Grail), becomes the kind of heresy that, even as recently as 2006, saw the Vatican insist that a warning be shown before the start of the movie The *Da Vinci Code*, citing it as a work of fiction.

To writer Marina Warner's understanding of the Christian Fathers, 'Sexuality represented to them the gravest danger and the fatal flaw; they viewed virginity as the opposite and conqueror, sadly failing to recognize that renunciation does not banish or overcome desire.' As sexuality is central to all of life, why would organizations like the church even try to seek to remove it? A possible answer lies in the very power of sexual energy. It's a power which can lead to ecstatic union between people and the divine, and crucially requires no intermediary priesthood. Embarrass people about their sexualities, vilify and demonize them, and you restrict the avenues through which people can have divine experiences. In effect you monopolize devotion, and the body ceases to be a temple unless sex is removed.

Like Christianity, Greek philosophy also attempted to remove the feminine. To negate the body, and its functions, was an attempt to make the body, like society, independent of a maternal lineage. The fact that as living, breathing, corporeal beings our existence is dependent on both the matter which comprises our bodies, and the matter that passes in and out of us in order to maintain them, is perhaps the greatest obstacle to the establishment of this masculine idea of self-sufficiency. Our reliance on water and food, with the requirement that they come out the other end, would have been shocking enough to a philosophy seeking to remove Mother Earth from its discourse. It was therefore left to other human needs – like love, sex and affection – to be curtailed and denied. If they had to happen, best they took place in private without any further discussion, which is how some people to this day imagine intimate relationships must operate. And in public they were berated. Acts like masturbation and menstruation were decreed polluting if not damnable, with all that viscous product leaking out of the body politic.

The division, cleaved at the most personal level, between the body (profane) and the mind (sacred) extended beyond sexuality to all manner of hygiene. Cleanliness was honored as next to godliness, with the assumption that spirituality must be so disembodied as to be astral. The intellectualizing of this fear of what is natural has been used to justify everything from chemical soap powder to circumcision. As feminists like Gloria Steinem understand, 'The real reason for female genital mutilation can be heard in the context of patriarchy: men must control women's bodies as the means of production and thus repress the independent power of women's sexuality.' During his-story, anything that could be associated with feminine Nature had to be cleansed. The natural, sexualized bodies of all sexes were the first to be scrubbed.

With religion and philosophy paving the way, it was then left to science to promote the bathroom, sewage system and chemical toilet as the sacred spaces of the secular age. The paranoia towards dirt has gone so far that today the Stanhope Hotel Apartments in America accommodate an inhabitant for every two to three bathrooms. Many of the problems of our age, such as pollution of air and water from synthesized chemical cleaners and the rise of autoimmune diseases according to the hygiene hypothesis, are rooted in his-story's institutionalized fear at what our bodies are capable of expelling.

Yet gardeners have long known the value of blood, fish, bone and horse manure as the best fertilizers. Urine is increasingly remembered as being great for compost heaps. Anyone who has encountered composting toilets knows the fear of human waste is revealed as ridiculous. Not only is there no repellant smell; the waste breaks down naturally enough to provide fertilizer for fruit trees and bushes. Those who face, rather than flee, their fears realize that the cycle works simply without any waste.

But the longstanding fear coming from a divided mind has established numerous psychoses around the base regions. We learn to despise those genital organs most intimately associated with sex because of their dual function: promoting orgasmic pleasure and evacuating shit, piss and menstrual blood. The early Christian writer, Tertullian, called women 'the gateway to the devil' and St. Augustine recoiled in horror at this commingling of the sexual and excretory organs when he said, 'We are born between feces and urine.' Menstruation, one of the most powerful bodily processes, connecting women with their bodies, the rhythms of the moon and the world, has become something to feel shamed by. By the 20th century, psychoanalyst Melanie Klein suggested that girls hide away the evidence of their first period because they identify with exactly this concept of contamination. To date, many women take the contraceptive pill 'back-to-back' to stop themselves ever bleeding. The legacy of disgust with menstrual flow has leaked all over his-story.

To see menstruation as a curse is far more common than to consider it an unexplored resource. Generations of social scientists have paid more attention to the words and actions of men than of women; thus the ethnographic record is overflowing with descriptions of men's fear, disgust and anger at menstruating women. In Native America neither women nor men viewed menstruation as shameful or unclean; rather it was powerful and magical. The negative view of menstruating women as polluting demons is mostly found wherever a hierarchical male priesthood controls religious ideology. What many tribal societies recognized was that within the dark fluids of menstrual and birthing blood resides the vital essence of the most feminine form of spiritual energy, and just before and during menstruation women experience their strongest healing and oracular powers. As a Muskogee holy man puts it, 'Men must take a sweat bath once a month while women are naturally purifying themselves to keep their medicine effective.' What the west limits as premenstrual syndrome (and treats as an illness) has, in other cultures, been respected as one of the most powerful moments in a woman's month.

According to the monotheistic theories of Judaism and Christianity, menstruation is a *curse* inflicted on women (together with the pain of childbirth) because of Eve's *original sin*. Over thousands of years, women have been taught to feel ashamed of the power of their bodies and been made to disguise the process behind closed cubicle doors. In many societies throughout this age, the scale of misogyny has led repeatedly to separate dwelling areas for menstruating women and edicts (issued by male priests) that a woman in her blood should come nowhere near a ritual because of her 'instability'. In addition, other prohibitions were issued against roles that women were traditionally able to take part in. In the hands of men, menstruating women were no longer allowed to hunt because men assumed that menstrual blood would overwhelm their power to kill. But as blood attracts animals, the taboo against hunting only makes sense as an excuse to disempower women. As poet, and menstrual historian, Penelope Shuttle says, 'Uterine blood would be a very potent "drag" for laying scent-trails' with huntresses using 'their powerful-magic menstrual blood as a trail'.

What writers like Bruno Bettelheim suggest, and what Freud didn't, was that such hostility to women might have been due to vagina or womb envy.

Across tribal cultures, some men would cut themselves with symbolic wounds to identify with the power of women and the Great Mother. This would often occur as a ritual associated with puberty to try and mirror the profound moment of a girl's first menarche (bleeding), but could often continue and might involve castration for those men willing to make themselves into females in order to share women's powers. Margaret Mead charted tribal societies where synthetic male menstruation (bloodletting for males) occurred. She suggested that the shedding of blood in secret by women gave rise to aggression and anxiety in many men, which accompanied the need for these men to demonstrate themselves superior to women, take charge of the ideology and the ceremonies, and perpetuate an idea that woman must suffer for her difference. So the men who were supposed to be students of these abilities in women, have, throughout the last age, become the proud and envious aggressors.

The lie behind the masculine attempt to separate body from mind is revealed when we consider the power of mental thoughts working with physical attraction, not least in the theatre of pornography. The myopic behavior of the masculine brain and male penis can develop, like bodily hair, from puberty onwards, finding ever more powerful, disturbing and complex scenarios of erotic charge. Possibly men tend towards imbalance in their understanding of sex because, unlike women, their genitals give neither bleeding nor babies: neither agony nor ecstasy. The masculine watches in horror, fascination and desire at the range of female sexuality; then it adjusts her according to how he thinks she should behave. This prescription of sexuality found expression during the epidemic of slavery, where throughout the 18th century British writers and artists constructed the orient and oriental as titles for the projection of their desires and fears. Pictures by the artist Gillray show the inversion of the permitted cultural sado-masochism of white master and black slave, with a female black slave becoming the sexual dominant of white settlers. But this fleshy fetishized idea of black harem woman, her physical attributes and character traits, was compiled by male European desire.

The attempt to erase women and sexuality from his-story has consistently failed, as the very people who were intended to be suppressed were figures of erotic appeal. But that hasn't stopped the masculine from trying. Where man couldn't control the urge by the marital bond or by paternal invective, he frustrated it with enforced chastity, subdued it through rape or rationed it within marriage – so long as a son was the outcome. As Mary Daly has powerfully documented, the forced burning of Indian widows, Chinese foot-binding, African genital mutilation, European witch burnings and modern American gynecology are all examples of men playing god with the female form across this patriarchal age. For many men it's the natural equivocation of woman, both sexual animal and maternal channel, that proves unmanageable. The Madonna/Whore split of the two Christian Maries becomes a complex. Challenged by multitasking, the masculine can only see one woman at a time. So woman is *either* the model of chastity whom he has married, *or* the model of depravity who exists in magazines and fantasies – whose identity as other people's daughters and sisters and wives doesn't limit the expansive list of perversions they seem, according to the objective masculine gaze, to be begging for.

The strength of aversion towards base sexual power is passed onto children by parents who themselves feel tainted by an ancient curse. Parents look on in confused shock as their offspring begin to show signs of sensual enjoyment, and reprimand with a force that only lets the children know they have stumbled on something terribly powerful but shameful. For woman, according to de Beauvoir, the inferiority complex takes the form of a rejection of her femininity. 'It is not the lack of a penis that causes this complex, but rather woman's total situation; if the little girl feels penis envy it is only as the symbol of privileges enjoyed by boys.'

Still the power of the sexual force does not diminish. Like damming a stream, water always finds a way. For some the power of sexual energy manifests as fetish, whereby the forbidden (taboo) becomes the worshipped (totem). Sexual pleasure is heightened by the involvement of acts, objects or roles that are forbidden. One of the grimmest illustrations of sexual repression is Jack the Ripper, whose evisceration of his victims' guts marks the crazed frenzy of someone overcome with the uncontrollable force of his (culturally forbidden) sexual urges. Though his identity remains debated (the painter Walter Sickett and the then Prince of Wales are both candidates), the mythology implies that after cleaning his tool, he returned to the kind of violently polite Victorian society that was so terrified of sexuality it covered up piano legs for fear of their potential to arouse.

In Indian philosophy, on the other hand, sex is encouraged to the extent there's even a manual, *the Kama Sutra,* to aid the practice of mutual pleasure. The Eastern concept of Tantra encourages love-making that allies the physical with the spiritual, turning our bodies into temples to be explored, touched, stimulated and celebrated. Kundalini Yoga and the Taoist energy arts of Qi Gong and Tai Chi accept and work with the enormous potential of these life-giving forces and make the practice about opening the lower center and leading the energy (in serpentine curves) up the channels and back down. The dance of the two energies, the masculine and feminine, yin and yang, are not forbidden, but encouraged. We have to start from the force in our lowest center, especially the one born in sexual attraction, if it is to lead up to the higher centers. In its natural essence this power becomes capable of transmutation and elevation, through sex as through dance and music. Like our attitudes to the waste from our bodies, sexual energy only becomes a problem when we fear and flee from it.

The dance of these masculine and feminine energies makes the shape of the two entwined serpents. It is the 'wand of Caduceus', the same image that decorates ambulances as a sign of healing, and prefigures the double helix of the contemporary genetic model. It is something the old alchemists understood, among them Isaac Newton who believed that the universe was instinct with life and spirit, in the feminine and masculine semen that was responsible for generation. Unlike the biblical creation story, the serpent needn't be damned as the root of evil but can instead become the demonstration of energetic power, coursing through the land and through our bodies. The suppression, distortion and imbalance of these energies can lead to sickness, but as Leanne Payne, author of *Crisis in Masculinity*, says, 'When man and woman are reasonably balanced within themselves they find "the sword between the sexes" removed.' It is the harmonizing of these energies that tends to health.

How we celebrate this energy (or otherwise) reveals how we treat our bodies and Mother Earth. Suppressing and demonizing our own bodily functions has only led to enormous rates of waste and sickness. The high levels of toxins that we use to self-medicate our way through stress-wrecked days reveals this disharmony as well as an increasing dissatisfaction with it. The scale of environmental pollution suggests we are only destroying our home and ourselves more as we find further ways to flee from what is inherent and necessary to the very condition of being alive.

According to the energetic system of chakras, the root energy center is dark: maroon, red, brown; intense earth colors as grounding as soil, as powerful as volcanic lava. To whiten them is akin to the many refining processes that refused to allow brown sugar on the tea tray, or commanded fine bone china instead of clay: an unnatural process that creates an untenable model of cleanliness as rare as an immaculate conception. Perhaps it's time to assess whether we need bleach, toilet ducks and yet more forests of lavatory paper. Perhaps we need to understand that the prevalence of brown as the color of soil explains why our toilets weren't ever meant to be white.

This Woman's Work

To recall the hunter/gatherer paradigm is to bring up the exchange between those who adventure in the hunt for supper and those who tend the camp. But the absolute decree that men perform the former and women the latter limits the possibilities of expression and excellence for all. The attributes of sex are a biological given, but gender is a product of historical process. In other words, the fact women bear children is due to sex; the habit that women nurture children is due to the cultural construct of gender.

During his-story, the work we've undertaken has been schematized. *Real* work has been the prerogative of man, while woman merely has things to occupy her that are sometimes tiring, but often not fully satisfying. That one is considered *real* while the other is dismissed as *not*, might go some way to explain why, during this age, boys have seldom been encouraged to knit. And while changes are undoubtedly afoot, there are still loud voices proclaiming traditional gender roles for the sexes. *The Mail on Sunday* launched an advertising campaign in 2008 depicting the difference between the sexes once again as battle. Men were on one side, kicking their footballs and commanding remote-control trucks; women on the other, hurling lipsticks and unleashing toy dogs. Peace, so the advert promised, was only possible on Sunday, when both sexes signaled a truce under their respectively gendered color supplements. Five thousand years of imbalance seem ready to drag into the foreseeable under this flagship tabloid.

It's no wonder that for many women over the last century, the arrival of machines has been celebrated. Juggling home, family, partner and, if they're lucky, a job and sense of self, might have been belittled by men, but the complexity of routine is eased when there are devices to help clean and cook. In place of domestic service, machines step in with the power of electricity to iron shirts and wash the dishes. They occupy the children and make the tea. There is no doubt that the weight of such work grows more burdensome the more isolated individuals become. Living in extended families and tribes enables the tasks to be shared, stimulating the individuals by not piling all the work upon them on a daily basis. Childcare can be spread around, and the socializing potential of young people growing up with other young people around them is impressive.

Yet it is in the traditional view of some occupations as woman's work that our culture has missed valuable opportunities. Cooking and cleaning are indicative of circular time, and according to masculine linear time, circularity has been written off as dull and pointless. These occupations have been stripped of value and derided. Yet such roles are crucial to the daily survival of the community, as certain other cultures have recognized. Wilma Mankiller was the first female chief of the Cherokee nation between 1985 and '95. According to the traditions of Cherokee culture, she emphasized a balance between the two genders and revived the tradition of *gadugi*: the coming together of men and women for the common good. In Mead's anthropological exploration of tribes in the South Seas, she found the assumptions that women are biologically more capable of enduring monotony, without psychic expense, to be without foundation. More often than not, she witnessed tribes in New Guinea where women share in the heavy, exacting spurts of work, and men share in the small routines of everyday life; and those in Samoa, where both men and women do heavy, exacting gardening and tiring fishing. Both climb, both carry, both alternate vigorous work with periods of quiet industriousness and long relaxing hours of singing and dancing.

Without due respect, it becomes easy to take the little tasks for granted and to create a system whereby food is consumed without gratitude, undermining its nutritional value. If child-raising is viewed by a dominant masculine ideology as mundane and boring then not only do boys and girls grow up to despise the circular tasks and whoever is assigned to them, but the idea of the sanctity of raising the next generation becomes similarly devalued. The extension of the logic that men are powerful and women are powerless unbalances the way communities are governed. Men assume it is their right to arbitrate and rule, and these roles are encouraged at the expense of others. The more fixed such divisions become, the more generations believe this is how it always was and how it always must be; the less capable individuals feel in adapting and challenging their positions, even when every ounce of them is pleading to take a different route. So girls are forbidden from taking the role of warrior, hunter and leader; and boys are scorned and derided for wanting to raise children, tend the stove and be part of the weaving of the community.

Many parents now see childcare as something to be handed over to others at the nearest opportunity. Many men still see their role as scant, if they've stuck around long enough to see the fruit of their loins arrive. For professionally successful women, like Rachel Cusk, the risk of giving birth is to witness a partnership split, so that where before the couple was living in a state of some equality, they now exist in a sort of 'feudal relation to each other'. She writes of her own experience of becoming a parent in *A Life's Work*, of the profound gulf between childcarer and worker, and suggests that few men 'would countenance the injury to their career to look after children' because to do so would be 'to risk the same loss of self-esteem that makes a career in motherhood such a difficult prospect for women'. It's a far cry from the society of Mundugumor, where Margaret Mead discovered that men permanently nurture and care for women and children, and each new generation of young males learns nurturing behavior. In many indigenous cultures, the child is raised witnessing and learning the tasks firsthand from both parents. In our culture, work conditions in many jobs do not encourage the knitting together of children, parenting and career. Children as a reality and prospect are sidelined as many women fear being overlooked at work if they take time out to give birth. Many male colleagues view the biological imperative of women to have children as a reason to sustain bigotry (they shouldn't be playing at boys' games in the first place, etc.), and even other women begin to disapprove, having opted to prioritize work over family. The polarity between serious business and child's play shows the imbalance in practice. Many men still resist entering what journalist Barbara Ellen calls 'chick-work'. Are they really put off by the thought of being perceived as unmanly, out of place, even suspicious? Or is it that 'the money isn't great, while the work is demanding but low-status'?

The longer we promote a gendered basis for occupation, the more generations will suffer. Our little people are the champions of the future. Their upbringing and care is central to the growing society of tomorrow. If raising them is seen as equally valuable with every other work, then the possibilities of generating a future of well-adjusted, confident and skilled adults becomes more likely.

Witi Ihimaera's novel *The Whale Rider* presents a young girl whose destiny is to take on the mantle of the tribe's founder Paikea, but who is frustrated by the gender-limited vision of her traditionalist grandfather. To his understanding, a girl could never lead a tribe. Conversely, but congruently, the story of *Billy Elliot* shows the struggle of a young boy to be allowed to dance in the face of the prescription of his father at what a *real* man's job must be. Whether girl, boy or transgender, the main opposition they face to their becoming is invariably a father; a man who has grown up with the cultural bias of his-story: that men must be in charge, undertaking violent struggle to keep the changing world fixed for the next generation of male rulers.

It is a start to suggest that boys and girls be allowed to follow their own path. But we can all benefit by encouraging ourselves to see worth in every task that forms the bedrock of our existence and that of the world we are charged with maintaining. The so-called 'woman's work' of the home offers profound learning and rewards for those who undertake it. Circular occupations ground us in the movement of time and help the development of key skills like patience, meditation and practice. They offer the chance to go deeper inside ourselves through these occupations. As Gandhi became the spiritual hero of occupied India, his daily work involved spinning yarn. This was not from an inability to dramatically alter the political state of his homeland, but out of awareness that the engagement with apparently simple and circular tasks brings its own rewards of contemplation and spiritual/personal connection. In addition, making equal worth out of the different, smaller, tasks might reward us more than we think. In the Balinese culture that she studied, Mead found that men and women work, pause to smoke, take a stroll, play with the baby, play a bit of music and fall back into the pattern of work again. This is an example of a tribe where there is no word for 'tired'.

Work once seen as *tedious* by a system that only placed value on the yang aspects of physically strenuous labor, can offer the chance to develop a state of no-mind, creative inspiration, spiritual connection and a greater awareness of living in the moment: as well as the more physically tangible and socially essential rewards of baking bread, spinning thread and inventing stories. It is increasingly these more feminine ways of working that have been subtly developing during the machine age. Philosopher Sadie Plant writes about this in her book about women and digital technology, *Zeros and Ones*. Automation has been matched by a feminization of the workplace; the more sophisticated the machines, the more feminine-minded the workforce becomes. The range of new technology, telecommunications and media has accompanied a collapse in the west of the demand for heavy industry, and in their place comes a need for speed, intelligence, and transferable interpersonal and communications skills. These skills are the ones best suited to the feminine way of working. With its language of nets and webs, it is no wonder that the digital age finds its most successful analogy with the traditionally feminine world of weaving.

The seed for this subtle resurgence took root from man's own delineation of tasks. Plant observes that

> Man once made himself the point of everything. He organized. She operated ... She did the jobs he considered mundane, often the fiddling, detailed, repetitive operations with which he couldn't be bothered; the dirty, mindless, semi-automatic tasks to which he thought himself superior.

The rise of increasingly complex and specialized machines has brought a return of these *mundane* tasks to the landscape of the modern world. They have always been working away, vital to us in a way that many male counterparts are only now beginning to glimpse. The challenge to the masculine dominant has spread throughout digital technology, with its equally valued components of zeros and ones, the binary code making every digital sound and image. Master copies lose their mastery: everything valued for its bulk finds itself overrun by micro-processings once dismissed as too small and insignificant to count.

To have contracted out the bulk of the ordinary tasks to factories and machines, as happened under the industrial revolution, was one of the major blows to families working together, although it empowered women to step out of the constraints of domestic patriarchal restrictions. Yet, the system of production and division of labor that developed and which has been exported round the world cannot stop at women merely succeeding under masculine terms. While it is this technological evolution accomplished by men that has emancipated the women of today, allowing women the chance to show themselves more than capable of stepping up to the challenges of man's work, it is not a long-term solution; as the environmental consequences of global industry and technological displacement remind us on a daily basis.

No one else needs to do the dirty work for us when such tasks are afforded value. In seeing some tasks as desirable and others as derogatory, subcontracting the latter out to others, we have become poorer, our skills fewer, and our potential for spiritual connection as well as practical survival, slimmer. Becoming reliant on machine-made food, we deny ourselves the vitality of eating what grows freshest and nearest to us. Having omitted the practice of crafting our daily needs, fixating instead on the final product, we have cauterized the process out of our lives. In making slaves of others and machines, we might imagine our lives easier, whereas they are becoming harder; pushed to run at unnatural speeds, polluting our most essential needs and trapping us in a sense of restless ennui.

So much modern work now requires travel and immersing ourselves for at least eight hours a day behind the controls of one machine or another. Much of it is adrenaline-dependent, without the physical undertaking that helps our bodies process the excess secretion of the hormone. And the content of what we are doing, furthering the spread of machine technology, leads us further from our home, our land and our kin. We are instructed to work across day and night, traversing time zones to the cost of our health, surrounded by artificial noises and lights, deprived of darkness and silence, and prone to Nature-Deficit Disorder, constantly surrounded by people with whom we have scant relationship. The products we work to develop serve little constructive use for the Earth or ourselves; indeed more often they are actively damaging.

The clothes we wear are not worn with a sense of achievement and worth, and therefore seem valueless and disposable. The financially cheap cost of the clothes belies the hardships that are heaped onto those who make them, whose distance from us is so great that we are easily able to ignore them. The tools we use are not valued, but are those cheapest and least durable, therefore tossed aside into the nearest landfill site at the first sign of no longer working. Food is swallowed while the packaging remains. We are managers, system operators, IT experts, statisticians, strategists and analysts – all of which generate no end of stress but little genuine, practical, life-affirming end product or fulfillment. Waste is now the biggest contribution we are making to the world. And with so little of real worth being undertaken, we face the saddest result of our attempt to scour the *tedious* jobs from our lives: a feeling of uselessness in ourselves and at those around us.

Circular tasks do not enslave us: they ground us, helping us move at a natural pace, enjoying each other's company and listening to the quieter voices of the world; allowing us more relaxation and depth, more play and sense of accomplishment. And to value them as such helps us value those of all sexes who undertake them. In the circle, the potter, weaver, healer and wood-worker all have inestimable worth. If we are to help our children's children reclaim their lives across the world, we could do worse than making sure all tasks undertaken are valued and respected equally.

Girl Boy, Boy Girl

When Elizabeth I led England against the Spanish Armada she faced a conundrum: how to be England's commander-in-chief and a woman? Her solution was to become man as well as woman, as she demonstrated at Tilbury when she said, 'I know I have the body of a weak and feeble woman but I have the heart and the stomach of a king.' Her strategy might have sprung from needing to convince her subjects that gender was no bar to power, but it also offered an insight into the complexity of gender, sex and sexuality. The idea of a woman containing both male and female characteristics was uncommon, far less common that the number of men cross-dressing on the London stage at the time, but Elizabeth needed to show she had the balls for war, even if they weren't physically hanging between her thighs.

The attempt to keep boys and girls in the simple gender boxes of their biological sex has returned time and again during this age: in Victorian Britain and in the contemporary strengthening of traditional mindsets in, among other places, conservative America and Iran. At the physical level, biology is irrefutable. The splitting of sexes into those with a vagina and those with a penis seems forever destined to lock us into the shape of our bodies. If we are female there is a strong cultural expectation that, despite the ability to sail round the world or compose music, we should give birth to children. And the combination of a nine-month gestation period, together with a child-nurturing period that outstrips that of other mammals, implies that women ought to stay at home like a production line for babies. The presence of a penis is widely seen as requiring us to compete and prove ourselves, beat the other males to the post or a pulp in getting our stick or a mate. It has also been used to justify everything from sloth and lack of emotional dexterity, to unbridled promiscuity and physical abuse. Here stand the biological determinants of our mother and father archetypes: the girl who never leaves the home and the boy who never does anything but.

Traditionally, these are the poles, and, like our planet's polar regions, it is so chilling at either extreme that not much life can be supported. The defense of these rigidities has given rise to a situation in modern America where, as shaman and writer Barbara Tedlock says, 'Whenever a hermaphroditic or intersexed baby is born in a hospital, physicians almost always perform surgery to correct the child's sexual ambiguity.' The appearance of the physically hermaphroditic has given them little status outside the freak show. And for everyone else, the rule has been simple: If you're in the shape of a man: be a man. If you're a girl: be a girl. Our impermeable masculine system has struggled to find the feminine flexibility, running a mile from the idea that things can be, and usually are, fuzzier than that.

Queen Elizabeth I is not the only person to have suggested that gender might be different from sex and have so vital a role in our individual psyches, tastes and make-up. Carl Jung, pupil of Freud, explored the territory of archetypes; profound models that infuse our psyches. He identified the existence of the anima and animus, a feminine and masculine spirit respectively, which live within the physical sculpture of our sex and which may veer wildly away from the truth of our genitalia. By the 21st century, gender has come to take its proper place as a subject for discussion, up there with sex and the third member of this trinity, which confuses and enriches the possibilities further: sexuality.

The differentiation grows more astounding, the more it is permitted and the more it permeates. The loss of established gender norms has, in the words of theorist Judith Butler, the effect of 'proliferating gender configurations, destabilizing substantive identity and depriving the naturalizing narratives of compulsory heterosexuality of their central protagonists: "man" and "woman"'. This sea-change ensures that anything claiming to be normal has become peculiar. So a married straight male journalist with a powerful feminine spirit has a sex change. John Morris becomes reputed travel writer Jan Morris, and she continues to live with her former wife until the law catches up with experience, and the civil partnership ruling of 2006 allows the two women the chance to legally honor their 30-year partnership by getting married again.

Wherever people fall within the parameters of man/woman, straight/ gay, masculine/feminine, the radical expansion of permitted options creates a spectrum where previously there was monochrome. Like interrupting a beam of light with a prism, there now emerge confident differentials embracing their choice and destiny to be, for instance, a masculine gay male, a feminine bisexual male, a masculine straight female, an androgynous bisexual transsexual. It helps us to see that gender is an act open to splitting, parody and those exaggerated exhibitions of the normal that, in their very exaggeration, reveal gender's illusive character. As a result of opening our eyes to an innately diverse world, the idea of life being made up of *either* feminine straight females *or* masculine straight males seems laughable and not a little pallid.

The availability of sex-change operations to match up spirit with sex is desirable for some and unthinkable for others. Either way, the emergence of transvestites and transsexuals smudges the boundaries even more. Many women would find it absurd to imagine the only way their resurgent power could be acceptable was by changing their biological sex. For many gay men in Iran (where, as the government reminds us, there are no gay men) the death penalty is a horrific incentive to change sexes. Homosexuality is banned there because apparently it 'disrupts the social order'. In 1983 Ayatollah Khomeini passed a fatwa authorizing people to have sex-change operations, providing 'a cure for people suffering from this problem': homosexuality. As a result, Iran has the highest number of male to female transsexual operations in the world second to Thailand (where religious and social conservatism is similarly intimidating). In 2008 Tanaz Eshashian made a film, *Be Like Others*, which explores why sex-change operations are seen as necessary in Iran. 'If you are a male with female tendencies, they don't see that as something natural or genetic. They see it as someone who is consciously acting dirty.' Ironically, in an attempt to limit the definition of what is natural, the Iranian authorities are widening the possibilities of sexual diversity further.

It seems the most natural way of being in the world is to allow the mix of these ingredients without repression. Yet there are still powerful forces from this outgoing age, driving to keep the feminine locked down under masculine control. Even some socially conservative women fall into the trap of oppressing themselves and their sisters, out of a belief shaped over thousands of years that the rules of the masculine are unquestionable. In the wake of Mrs. Thatcher, it seems that capitalism allows a degree of masculinity in women, if for no other reason than for them to shore up its system. At no stage does it permit young men to see anything worthwhile in embracing the feminine. This is why, in the words of Julie from Ian McEwan's *The Cement Garden*, 'Girls can wear jeans and cut their hair short, wear shirts and boots, cos it's okay to be a boy ... but for a boy to look like a girl is degrading because you think being a girl is degrading.' So established is the supposed undesirability of the feminine that even many men who identify as gay can often be heard chorusing that they like a man 'to be a man'.

Homosexuality has been continually condemned in the context of monotheism, portrayed as nothing short of *evil* because it is contrary to heterosexuality and reminds us that our sexuality supports a feminine path. Chronicler Gerald of Wales expressed Christianity's established views on the matter in his 12th-century discussions of the Welsh; blaming their subjugation on their sins, particularly the 'wicked and detestable vice of homosexuality'. The edicts of Christianity against homosexuality can still be virulent in the modern age. In 2000 the Pope called homosexuality 'objectively disordered' and 'contrary to natural law' and in 1999 the Congregation for the Doctrine of the Faith issued a statement proclaiming that 'homosexual acts are always objectively evil'. The antimony facing gay people in vigorously Christian places such as contemporary Uganda feels Medieval. Even in 2011, two men are ejected from a pub in London's gay district, Soho, for kissing on a date.

Writer Tariq Ali says, 'Islam's strictures on homosexuality are almost pathological ... the effeminate man and the boyish woman are both denounced as deviants in revolt against the laws of God. In this respect, at least, the three monotheisms are in agreement.' Despite this, one of the heroes of Islam is the 13th-century Sufi poet Rumi, who was attracted to, found inspiration in, and dedicated his mystical love poetry to another man: Shams of Tabriz. There are many interpretations of their encounter, but however they met, Shams and Rumi became inseparable. In various poems, the spiritual nature of their love is given added body. In 'Music Master' Rumi writes:

When I am with you, we stay up all night.
When you're not here, I can't go to sleep ...
I want to hold you close like a lute,
So we can cry out with loving.

In 'The Vigil' he says:

Shams, so loved by Tabrizians, I close my lips.
I wait for you to come and open them.

And in 'The Music':

I saw you last night in the gathering,
But could not take you openly in my arms,

So I put my lips next to your cheek,
Pretending to talk privately.

Despite this, many scholars of Rumi are unwilling even to acknowledge the love between the two men.

A representative instance of how homosexuality still upsets, especially young men, is the case of Majid, a 13-year-old British Muslim and one of the interviewees in Libby Brooks' *The Story of Childhood*. What would he do if one of his friends told him that he thought he was gay? Brooks asks. 'He points to his father's walking stick ... "Take that," he says deliberately, "bring it down on his head ... It's WRONG!!!" he shrieks. "God made man and woman for a reason, not man and man. It's going against the rule of nature."'

Yet it seems Nature has other ideas. In 1999 a book called *Biological Exuberance* by Bruce Bagemihl was published, successfully charting nearly 500 animal species that engage in homosexual behavior. For many, the argument that homosexuality is unnatural could finally be tossed overboard to turn into something more useful for coral. The world's wildlife may be depraved, but we would be hard-pushed to call it unnatural. Yet despite the growth of the gay movement and queer identities, there is still an enduring negative attachment, best demonstrated by the linguistic somersaults the word 'gay' has done; now resting in the hands of many young men, anxious to find some hold on the crumbling edifice of unbalanced masculinity, who equate it with 'shit'. Homophobia, like racism and sexism, may be the sort of intolerance that rises up when external pressures are felt, but, like institutionalized racism, homophobia is written through his-story like letters through a stick of rock. The justification that many homosexuals are required to make – to try and build a sense of self-worth in the face of a society that, even when it accepts them, can't quite see what they're for (continually, for there is never an end to coming out) – prevents them from clearing their own internalized homophobia. Whether from the conservative sections of Jewish, Islamic or Christian society, in terms of acceptance of other sexualities, fear and hatred run deep. As Alice Walker says of life in America, 'How sad now never to see men holding hands, while everywhere one looks they are holding guns.'

It is therefore something of a surprise to find a wholly different story in many tribal and ancient cultures, for which monotheism was no friend either. In a number of traditions, the ideal gender may be embodied in an androgynous deity, a creator with a shifting gender, or even a two-gendered culture hero, such as Ometeotl in Aztec cosmology who was the self-generating goddess of duality. In many North American tribes, male and females who showed a powerful alternatively gendered spirit, or who had attraction to those of the same sex, were called 'two-spirit'. They were seen as being remarkable individuals with extraordinary powers, and their welcome into the circle was guaranteed. More often than not, such individuals became the shamans of the tribe. The social respect given to such people meant that to partner them was one of the highest honors. Female shamans often took on male characteristics and modes of dress and female partners. Conversely male shamans often took female characteristics and dress and male partners. As Barbara Tedlock says, 'The most powerful shamans of either sex work with both masculine and feminine forms of energy' in a transformation of gender or frequent gender bending and blending. The two-spirited might also relate to those whom Alice Walker refers to as 'two-headed'. She explains that

> Two-headedness was at one time an actual physical condition and two-headed people were considered wise ... Two-headed people, like blacks, lesbians, Indians, 'witches', have been suppressed, and in their case, suppressed out of existence ... [but] rootworkers, healers, wise people with 'second sight' are

called 'two-headed' people.

Across continents there are indigenous words for such people who encompass more fully the hermaphrodite or multi-gendered. In Navajo they are called the *Nadlech*; in Crow, the *Bote*; and in Lakota, the *Winkte*. People of multi-gender are also afforded valuable stories within the oral telling of the pantheons. Among the Navajo, the survival of humanity was said to depend upon the inventiveness of two-spirited deities. Among the Zuni, legend tells of a battle between the agricultural and hunting spirits in which a two-spirited deity brought peace to the warring parties. In Maori culture the *Takatapui* are those who have an intimate companion of the same sex. Maori society was tolerant and accepting of diversity and difference, especially those based on sexuality and sexual expression, unlike the colonizers from our own culture who eradicated stories of Maori sexuality from the canon. And it was the French fur traders arriving in North America who coined the term *Berdache*, attempting to sum up the complexities of two-spirit people by reducing them to a word which means 'those who practiced anal intercourse'.

In many prehistoric Goddess cultures, men who demonstrated what we would refer to (clumsily) as 'gayness' were often temple priests; their femininity a blessing connecting them with the divine, not an embarrassment to be hidden, excused or corrected with electroshock treatment and bible classes. With the coming of patriarchy, the rules were altered. In Ancient Sumer around 2100 BC, Eunuchs would have maintained some of their erstwhile privileges, succeeding within the new terms of patriarchy because they were seen as having no loyalty to military and aristocratic families, and no dynasty of their own to protect. But unlike their valued position within Goddess-based societies, they were respected only for the ease with which they could be killed. In China during the Ming dynasty, Eunuchs were often relied upon by the Emperor, but were frequently belittled by the *virtuous* aristocratic officials who tended to be jealous of their advancement. In contemporary Mexico, *Muxe* men are not referred to as homosexuals but constitute a separate category based on possessing feminine gender attributes. People perceive them as having the physical bodies of men but different aesthetic, work and social skills from most men. In Hindu culture the Kama Sutra talked of a third sex, like the *Hijra*: male singers in saris who would arrive at social events and sing for pennies. It is only recently that the *Hijra* have begun to see themselves worthy of respect, rather than being considered a social embarrassment necessitating hasty paying off. Across the world, whether named Riot Girls, Butches, Femmes, Lady Boys, Dykes, Fags or Banjee Boys, there is a growing acceptance of fuzzy genders and an acknowledgment that these people have always been here; mute witnesses to a story written by their detractors.

It has been a struggle for sexualities that differ from the common to be permitted, let alone celebrated, over the last 5,000 years. Yet as the circles return, the alleged negative can no longer be banished. Even to see one sort as positive and the other as negative is to miss the recipe for diversity that other indigenous cultures understand. These sets of opposites are different from the dichotomies his-story issues, because they are interrelated rather than contrary. As transgender doctor and writer Joan Roughgarden says, 'Our species isn't divided into two classes, normal and different. Our species is naturally a rainbow of normalcies in every bodily detail.' As with animal diversity, the facts of cultural diversity in gender and sexuality are unexpected and mutating. No gene is king, no body type reigns supreme, nor is any template universal in this 'cacophonous cellular democracy'.

The young best demonstrate the wealth of the spectrum. Unselfconsciously bisexual, often androgynous and defying boundaries as hurriedly as they are erected, they flirt with, swim through, switch between and flick past the laborious border-posts of identity, in a manner most similar to the shamans of ancient times. Even the concept of a man with a feminine spirit has to be flexible enough to cover the infinite variety of radical transsexuals, gay drag queens, camp television presenters, bisexual pop stars and the occasional 6-foot-6 straight rugby player with a penchant for braided tiebacks.

The feminine shape of the circle, when applied to society, draws everyone together equally, regardless of gender/sex/sexuality configuration. The powerful benefit of this approach is to celebrate diversity and encourage individual excellence in whatever guise it emerges. The circle is made stronger when all parts of it are in their power. There is a sense that we are approaching a time when sexualities, like genders and sexes, can be embraced in their multiplicity and diversity; where children can feel their first sense of sexuality without fear of abuse or violation and where variants of gender are once more seen as a blessing and a boon to the circle; where everyone's power is encouraged, however many toes, or heads, they have.

Dispirited Youth

If you want an indication of where his-story has brought us, look to the children. This age has developed an institutional schizophrenia based on the binary of good and evil and our children are not exempt from it. They are elevated as innocent and in danger, and at the same time they are demonized as feral and out of control. The most newsworthy accounts of childhood today involve a recurrence of sickness and death. Knife and gun crime, suicide, alcohol and drug problems, dangerous levels of obesity, stress and depression, extreme relationships with body image, desperate consumption and a devout worship of the most material icons. And they're just following the example we're giving them.

The division between boy (*good*) and girl (*bad*) grinds on: his-story is taught at school, boys' stories are given currency for both genders, while the feminine is dismissed and ridiculed. The emphasis on boys' books in class, from books written by men to masculine theories of the world like science and history, means a dangerous cost in feminine self-esteem to children of all genders and sexes. It is unsurprising that when children eventually occurred as the subject of theorists, from Rousseau in the 18th century to Spock in the 20th, they were spoken of solely in the masculine.

During the height of Christianity the edict of *original sin* meant that children were frequently discussed as the product and carrier of *sin*. The young were born *damned*, further proof (according to his-story) that the fallen world was a recurring error in need of correction. The one exception was the Baby Jesus, belief in whom as the son of God was the only possible way for such inherent *sin* to be absolved. The emergence of Protestantism, aligned with industrial capitalism, prompted an acceptance of children, provided they became useful and productive members of the vast machine. As if to make up for the *sin* of their being, they were set to work. Books, and later magazines, appeared praising the virtues of duty and discipline, where the standard villain was an idle child. Children were seen as a separate entity needing rights to protect them from the de-familiarized workplace, and schooling to train and control them. From the 19th century onwards, children were more excluded from the crucial arenas of life. With a pattern set from the Victorian era of mass schooling, learning was conditioned as a restrictive process of knowledge assimilation and repetition.

The splitting tendency of his-story then switched to the innocent child *versus* the corrupt adult. The former was seen as requiring tuition, guidance and control to ensure his transformation into the normal (white, heterosexual, masculine) man, who would take up the reins of Empire. Physical discipline was seen as part of the process of character building, helping them keep their upper lips stiff. To spare the rod was to spoil the child, and in all the descriptions of spoiling, associations with the feminine were chronically unavoidable. Despite beatings, emotional silencing, institutional gender inequality and the now well-known passage of children down pits and up chimneys, childhood began to be romanticized as a lost land, a place of angelic innocence and wistful regret that could never be revisited.

If there is now a panic around children, at its root is the frenetic ideal of childhood innocence mixed with terror at what might stem from its corruption. The enduring power of this myth of innocence can be seen in the last few decades as fashion models become younger, and surgery and chemical injections are used to make the old look teenage. But matching this is a sense that young girls need to rapidly turn into women. So Lolita grows up only to retreat into her youth. This is the insane model girls are given of what it means to be a woman. The ideal child of the modern age follows the example of a pre-school beauty queen in America. She is made up beyond her years as if she's been fast-tracked into adulthood, with its designer wardrobe and priorities of greed and manipulation. In the billion-dollar industry of beauty pageants, over a hundred thousand children under 12 are encouraged to conform to a male idea of sexuality in order to feel productive. It is in performing convincingly at what society expects its women to be that girls learn about what roles they must assume in adult society. Feminist Naomi Wolf observes, 'The problem with linking standardized notions of sexualized beauty to self-esteem is that it doesn't present young girls or adult women with many choices.' Our young girls are finding their only sense of victory conforming to the authority of men.

And one of the most horrific by-products of this artificial cult of innocence in children is pedophilia. Venerating youth, making it appear as untroubled as the pre-lapsarian Garden, is to make it desirable. Baby-smooth skin is capable of making us pant with desire because smoothness signifies nothing at all and thus does not interfere with our projections. James Kincaid, who has written about the adult relationship with the desired child, and been accused of supporting pedophilia as a result, suggests: 'We are told to look like children, if we can and for as long as we can, to pine for that look ... we are instructed to crave what is forbidden, a crisis we face by not facing it, by becoming hysterical.' The victims of child abuse, murder and abduction, such as 6-year-old American beauty queen JonBenet Ramsey in 1996, bring to the surface both the horror at how successfully a child can be constructed as a sexual being and our guilt at the pleasure we take in such a sight. As most of us remember from our own experience in that transitory state, children are extraordinarily sexual beings, who flirt and seduce and explore their own and others' bodies. If we are to dispel the abuse that can grow from our fixation with the untouched child (as arbitrary as the idea of *original sin* that made it the contrary), it would help to consider our children as sexual and sensual beings in their own right, rather than the empty vessels of an adult gaze waiting to have meaning deposited onto them.

As children are the recipients of the culture they are born into, what are they learning? Excessive materialism looms large, as young children find their homes awash with plastic toys. Material divisions are entrenched, and conspicuous consumption matters nowhere so much as in the playground, where the young hunger for power and find it in material labels that denote status. Yet at a time of increasing affluence and material provision, children are unhappier than ever, and getting more so. The idea of contentment with less runs contrary to the industry of commercialism, powering towards the untapped market of the young, and seeming, in the words of Brooks,

> like a monstrous behemoth, pushing sex and saturated fats, creating a generation of obese, promiscuous, celebrity-obsessed automatons, dependent on brands for identity, bullying the poor few who cannot afford the right trainers, unable to appreciate gratification that is anything other than instant.

So in the face of limited places for the ultimate prize of mass materialism, children are learning to compete, inducted into schools that begin to test their abilities from the age of 6, and encouraged to separate girl from boy and judge accordingly. Comparison also promotes a sense of relative deprivation and inadequacy, affecting interpersonal relationships and self-esteem. The British education system sets child against child in an endless quest for *standards*, and schools themselves compete for scarce resources.

The currency of money under the rule of capitalism has done away with every other value, rendering environmental and ethical concerns irrelevant in the race to get 'mo' paper'. Masculinity is taught to be favored; a spiritual dimension ridiculed or appropriated by monotheistic religion and made the tool of conflict. The gift of the feminine is evident only by its absence. The children of today are more aware than ever of the division between rich and poor, between the desirable heterosexual and the gay homosexual. And, adding weight to the 2006 Department for Education and Schools report that said there was a strong case for 'institutional racism in schools', the idealized child is (still) white, blond and middle class; not only invested with more humanity, but emblematic of the social order. Those who don't fit the image are banished from the public eye or permitted only token status.

More children now grow up in or around a city. Their independence and mobility is limited through fear; they feel excluded from public spaces and face more time imprisoned at school. Most children now associate anywhere outside their front door with danger, and fewer children than ever are encouraged to play in Nature. Growing up separated from Nature makes urban children less confident to engage with or value it when older. Instead they choose the concrete streets, creating their own danger with gang alliances, guns and drugs; mapping the world as solely human; more familiar with the shape of a Dalek than a barn owl; at one with machines; looking for their stars not in the sodium-lit and satellite-hung skies but on the magazine shelves of tormented celebrities. In panicking about the state of the world, we have locked our children away from it. And we wonder why they're not happy.

The oft trotted-out African proverb reminds us that it takes a village to raise a child. Yet in our culture the opposite is true, with some single parents encouraged to raise a village as a practical way out of poverty. Parenting is left to television, as Lisa and Bart Simpson remind their father. And while much has been made of the negative impact of DVDs, games and TV programs on children, nowhere is it observed that our society has welcomed television as a catch-all nanny and time-occupier.

There is a lacuna around puberty, with both school and parents believing it is the responsibility of the other to do the raising. Rates of suicide around bullying reflect keenly that without a spiritual education of togetherness and unity, the weak will be picked on and picked off by the physically brutal. If childhood continues as an experience of disempowerment, perhaps it shouldn't come as a surprise that some children misuse the only power they hold: over each other.

As this is a tale of how his-story has sown its seed, perhaps the most revealing specimens come in the shape of our young men. His-story has repeatedly taught us to value the masculine at the expense of the feminine. Nowhere is this clearer than in the interstitial zones of poverty-wrecked estates and postcodes that provide a new moniker for many urban experiences. 'Gangland' is the ghetto of the modern age. Like its young, it was raised by Margaret Thatcher and unbridled capitalism. It was told there was no such thing as society, learned that money was the only currency and that there was no moral code as to how it could be gained. But its distant ancestors are the army generals and the warrior kings who across his-story have shown that the only way to command respect was through violence and brutality.

In 2008, after a year of repeated violence by children on children, 'John Heale' wrote *One Blood: Inside Britain's New Street Gangs*. He found that killing was about respect because to lose respect was to jeopardize yourself. Faced with a mindset that wouldn't have looked out of place 5,000 years ago, the young engage with each other like armed poker players, incapable of sticking or folding. The only way situations can be resolved is through violence. It's the young who don't have the power, who dare to kill and be killed, because they stand to gain the most by enforcing their reputation. At one level there is a traditional and masculine hierarchy to their interrelation, with 'shotters' working for 'youngers' working for 'elders' working for 'faces'. But Gangland is neither organized nor legitimate and so there is fluidity to the roles, as individuals are relocated to prison, and territorialism and bloodlines work sometimes with, sometimes against, the hierarchy.

At the same time as politicians and commentators in the UK talk of a broken country, it needs to be remembered that in 2006 half of all murdered children were killed by a parent. The apprenticeship for many gang members is served in the home. If you are constantly on the alert for danger, and equate any show of emotion with violence, you are damaged in such a way that serves as an ideal preparation for gang life. You become a machine. Brutalized into territorialism, you see only danger when you look outside.

This mentality of groups of men fearfully asserting their control through force is central to his-story. It's no wonder that, in Gangland, gang rape can be excused with the scant justification of 'man's got needs'. In such a homo-social environment, men delineate between *hos* and *wifies*, marking the former as the women a man *owns* to share among his friends. Gangland is nothing new. It's how at the most extreme end of the scale during this age men have permitted themselves to behave. It might appall some to think of 10-year-olds having the capacity to be hitmen, stoking themselves on packed skunk spliffs and grime, before focusing their energy into pure rage and heading out to 'merk' someone. But isn't that what the assassins of Persia used to do, before carrying out the orders of their male superiors?

Like countless men before them, these young people are desensitized to acts of violence. They have learned to bottle up their rage and never show emotion; bereft and dismissive of the more feminine tools to deal with the pain they have suffered. They are at war, and the same traits that they display can be seen in soldiers coming back from war zones: anti-social behavior, aggression and hyper-vigilance. War is the most enduring model that shows how, over millennia, men have been trained to exhibit only their masculine attributes at the expense of the feminine.

What disturbs us is that the troops have got younger and it is now the children who carry the weapons. Religious extremism is not shielded from the young, and images of babies in Palestine and Israel being strapped with bombs and taught how to fire guns are only one aspect of a situation that sees the young and dispossessed being summoned to the aid of desperate fundamentalism. Before the Israeli army's temporary disengagement in 2005, the Gaza mental health program believed that the majority of local youngsters were suffering emotional problems as a result of the conflict. In early childhood this manifested in speech disorders, bedwetting or uncontrollable crying. But as the children grew older, their fear and distress distorted into rage.

In 2007 the 'Children's Tsar', Professor Sir Al Aynsley-Green, warned that the demonization and lack of empathy for young people was becoming a major issue for England. Camila Batmanghelidjh, founder of the charity Kids' Company in South London, reminds us that for many youngsters, their emotional coldness is the experience of growing up in abusive environments: 'A child who has been terrorized and neglected isn't going to feel threatened by punishment.' And indeed for children working their way up the Gangland ladder, prison is not so much a deterrent as a rite of passage. To claim we need to get 'back to basics' is to fail to see how the current outrage is merely the latest example of hyper-masculinity at work. Gangs such as the Muslim Boys openly reference organized religion to justify their actions, taking a passage from *the Qur'an* (Sura 8 – where Mohammed robs a set of caravans) to validate any action as long as it is followed by a trip to the mosque.

It is an irony that for all the talk of a father god in monotheistic religions, absent fathers are cited as one of the main reasons for the spread of gangs. With a father gone, and a mother trying to hold the home together, the young teenager finds his protection with an elder, who inducts him into a Gangland where men rule and only the physically toughest can join. As Beatrix

Campbell wrote in her work *Goliath*, once a boy had entered adolescence,

> What alternative way of being could attract him? … his *mother* … she could not be his role model … What she did was take care of people. What all the other men in his life – his father, his uncle, the brotherhood who threw bricks at the buses, the police, the court – promoted was what he himself now perpetrated, simple force.

But there is another absence in this territory, a spiritual gap in the heart of Gangland, with nothing to believe in and no one positive to emulate. It is no wonder that gangs predominate in areas of the country that are more heavily urbanized, where there is a far more longstanding history of poverty, without Nature and respected narratives of the feminine to nourish and nurture.

How can the feminine be welcomed when it has been so concertedly demonized? Mothers have been repeatedly made scapegoats for the tragedies of our young. They are condemned for being single parents and teenage mothers, for embracing feminism and absenting themselves from the traditional zone of the home. They are seen as the fault-bringers: ushering children through in the first place, giving them their psychological problems, nagging or smothering or abandoning them. When it comes to the potential role of men to be caring, nurturing and present, the hypocrisy is deafening. For a man to 'do the right thing' in regard to one's family is for him to lose status among his fellow men. Female parental absence is blamed, and seldom is the male role scrutinized. It's as if the man is excused involvement, unless he's training a boy to kill.

The threat of today's children can be seen in films like *Eden Lake*, which posits the latest demon as a 'trackie'-wearing youth, on a bike and with a dog. But half a century ago our culture had already found that to separate children from adults was to give rise to dark fears about what the 'little devils' may be up to. While the separation between child and adult was intended to afford children time to develop before taking up the mantle of economically productive units, the emergence of the teenager in 1950s America saw an adult panic at what these out-of-control creatures wanted to do. Stanley Cohen observed in 1972 that subcultures like Teddy Boys, Mods and Rockers, Skinheads and Hippies have all occupied a constant position as social 'folk devils'. These adolescent groups symbolize social change and threaten the logic that, given time and schooling, children will grow up to be the sort of people their parents want. As a result, a new genre of horror story emerged in the 1960s, with the *evil* coming out of the cradle. *Village of the Damned, Rosemary's Baby, The Omen, The Bad Seed, The Exorcist* – to name a few – all showed children to be the devil incarnate.

Few examples of dispirited youth struck as powerful a note as the killing of 2-year-old James Bulger in the UK in 1993. His murder by Jon Venables and Robert Thompson reflected both the absence of society as an inclusive and compassionate body, the absence of a spiritual heart, and the plight of material poverty to inflict damage on the next generation and beyond. What rose up from the much-publicized story was the readiness of this country's prurient, but somehow non-culpable, culture to condemn the two boys as *evil*. Rather than consider the welfare of every child as the responsibility of all, it seemed easier to condemn them. While *blame* was a much-touted word, far more scarcely heard was any talk of responsibility.

We are projecting the worst onto our children. Having once considered them the latest vessel of sin, then swinging to see them as a benchmark of perfect purity, we would now genuflect in front of them, had we not sold off our souls to science. Like the killer at the end of *Eden Lake*, with the only scientific evidence of murder deleted from his phone and the victim's shades put on as a mark of supremacy, he stares at his (and our) soulless selves in the mirror. With our spiritual core gone, he is merely following the adult example in feeling unrepentant and untouchable. Western materialism has removed the very part of him that might understand the law of karma and offer him the gift of remorse. He is the perfect example, not of wild youth, but of the masculinized system that has seen this island, in the words of Jeanette Winterson, 'leveled to this wasteland through the making of a Stone God and then by his destruction'. In the spiritual vacuum we have all co-created, there is no consequence to our actions. It's like *The Picture of Dorian Gray*, without the picture.

Yet somewhere far away from our atomized society, where children plug themselves into near-ubiquitous screens, perfecting the destruction of digital worlds in tandem to the environmental devastation of our own, a small idea persists: that children may be raised in Nature with actual humans around them, not through online chatrooms from which you disconnect when you're bored; that animals and plants are active companions and guides rather than senseless food; that there are more roles for girls and boys than the models of hookers and gangsters; that everyone is looking out for you, not just the drunken half-eye of the parent not yet managing to look after himself; that parenting itself is undertaken by an extended web of adults and other children, not just the tenuous and strained couple who may have already fractured.

In Mead's detailing of childhood in Samoa, she found a less sexually repressed society, free of shameful taboos and accepting of erotic experimentation. Children were raised by parents, elder siblings and a large and mutually supporting clan. They learned the tasks necessary for survival alongside their elders, where play was so central to life it did not command a different word. In Martin Prechtel's memoir of life in a Guatemalan village, the children take great pride in helping support their community as soon as they are able (around the age of 6 or 7). In his TV series *Tribe*, Bruce Parry came across 4-year-old Batana in the

Mongolian Steppes:

> To him, play was copying his father and learning the skills of life … When his dad was chopping wood, he'd be doing it too … When Puruhan was cooking, he would be right beside her, replicating her every move. He rarely smiled, and never at me. I had no obvious skills to copy: I got the impression he thought me a bit of an idiot.

If we don't want our children to turn into idiots, we have to stop giving them this example to follow.

What other cultures have practiced, and what we would benefit from remembering, are some of the most basic ways of being: to live in community, to share child-raising and other tasks, to view both the masculine and feminine as equally important, to feel supported. We do not need school so much as to learn how to live lightly with the Earth, following the wisdom of plants and animals, in tune with the day and seasons. We need a purpose in life and we need to value each member as having vital and unique gifts that help everyone. We need to remember ways to deal with suffering and loss that do not see repression leading to violence. We need to remember, as Sue Gerhardt has shown, what facilitates a massive burst of connections in the growing brains of our children. We need not less tolerance, compassion and play, but more. We need spiritual connection. We need, in a word, love.

As pressing as the need to help our children is, we have another child to think of: the one inside us. All of us have been born into his-story and born into the closing installment, like the leading carriage pulling a thousand caravans of pain, blame, suffering and guilt in its wake. Growing up within his-story will have marked every one of us, and finding a space where our inner child can grow and heal, reclaim the excitement and fun of the world with imagination and an innocent wonder, is vital. To emerge through the physical process of life with the ability to live child-like is to restore beauty and possibility to the world. To forego this process, denying the point of it, yet ranting and screaming and whining at the apparent unfairness and inadequacy of the world, is to reclaim not the child-like but the *childish*; expectant on some greater power to peer into the pram and replace the toys we've thrown out.

Our children may be facing some of the most demanding psychological and emotional hurdles laid down over millennia. But facing them they are. I feel the souls incarnating now are some of the oldest and wisest there are, and in their rapid grasp of technology and ability to process this last age and its messages, they demonstrate that wisdom. To help us at this time of transition we need the best. These children seem to be increasingly aware of what's going on and display character traits that overwhelmingly challenge the centuries-old understanding of many of their elders. The increased levels of sensitivity among them to over-processed foods and to the shortcomings of the institutions of education and government make them likely to begin from a much younger age to practice alternative forms of living. Despite the adult world's attempts to smother them, these souls are fast learners, and this challenges the orthodoxy that our numerical elders are necessarily wiser. Their rejection of longstanding concepts and models of behavior can be threatening to those who believe such models to be unchanging. But who better to have working on everyone's behalf than people with this kind of clarity?

And we need them, because this world they are born into is everyone's problem and needs all of us in our power in order to heal. So how are we going to do it? How are we going to reclaim our power and make the steps necessary to remember a relationship with the rest of life that is harmonious, nurturing and fun?

I'll give you a clue ... press 'Play'!

Making Monsters

If we're going to help make the world less monstrous, we need to begin by looking in the mirror. The dark mirrors of the big and small screens already give us monsters, showing us everything from clone wars to zombie armies. We have monsters of the sea, monsters of machines and monsters in space. But whatever the setting, the ever-present Bad Wolf is always somewhere outside us, over there.

One of the most iconic representations of a monster to come out of this last age has been Nature. All of her. The natural world has been vilified, from dragons sleeping in wells, to trolls lurking under bridges. While science has repeatedly negated the existence of such fabulous creatures, the microscope has managed to turn domestic bacteria and fleas into giant horrors with too many legs; ensuring the horror is still present, lurking not under our bed but in it, for which our savior is the trusted chemical spray. But in making monsters of our world, we have become alienated from the place that's supposed to be safest, without helping ourselves work on the ugly characters that squat within our own beings. Don't go outside, the warning sounds, for that's where the wild things are.

According to some of the most powerful stories of this last age, Nature is regularly portrayed as the enemy. Her most enduring symbols – women and serpents – find their representation at the beginning and end of *the Bible* as the ultimate monsters. In the Greek myth of the gorgons, Medusa manages to be both at once. And the beast of all beasts (the Christian devil in the guise of the Greek god Pan) manages to make a demon of most of the animal world. The prevalence of menacing forests, vigilant wolves, desolate moors, killer seas and jagged rocks, continues to paint our living planet as something nightmarish and insatiable, waiting for us to stray from our little huts so it can gobble us up. The poster for the film *Jaws* sums up the terror we feel towards our existence: we are a lone swimmer, unaware of the great, tooth-stuffed mouth surging upwards from the depths.

One of the first stories of this age, *The Epic of Gilgamesh*, presented the task that would become only too familiar: to kill the hideous monster once and for all. For Gilgamesh the hero, that monster was the nature god Humbaba, guardian of the cedar wood. The forest was both a real forest and a home of natural spirits, and, as its protector, Humbaba was a powerful divinity. The need for timber to build the new cities of his-story was the motive for Gilgamesh's expedition into the woods; he wished to display his power by building great walls and temples. But cutting it down had not been admitted as a political ambition because the wood was sacred. So Humbaba became *evil,* and Gilgamesh got the timber, as well as the glory for playing the heroic dragon-slayer.

The tale of a monster-thwarting hero recurs in *The Mabinogion,* in *Beowulf* and most enduringly for the English, with their patron, St. George. As well as rewarding material power to the successful knight, whether wood for building or ownership of the princess he's rescued, all these tales repeat the idea that the monster is separate from us and that the only solution is to hack at it with a sword.

The association between Nature and dragons can be seen clearly in the description of 'dragon lines', energy currents that serpent-weave across the land. In the UK such lines could be called 'leys' and in Chinese, *lung-mei*. The Welsh recognized the majesty of the dragon by depicting its image on their flag. In China the dragon chiefly represents the principle of fertility which waxes and wanes with the seasons of the year. In Britain, places associated with the dragon legend appear always to coincide with sites of ancient sanctity. But as monotheism and the rule of men developed, so Nature was seen repeatedly as needing to be slaughtered, so the slayer and the dragon came to represent the opposing principles of *good* and *evil.*

Of course there aren't dragons now. There aren't that many trees left, either. The success of successive generations of people following his-story and *conquering* Nature has seen the entire world brought to a state of profound ill-health. Such has been the consistent propaganda against Nature that most of us feel safer in the cities. No matter how alarming the state of the countryside, how ruinous the waste-strewn verges, and how easily sawn-through the factory-farmed pine trees, there are still the voices of those wielding the chainsaws that say Nature's just getting what she deserves. Irrespective of the calls to understand our home before we destroy her, unpersuaded by the idea that Nature's health mirrors our own, deaf to the sense that the richness of her wilderness ensures our wealth, the fear persists that Nature is monstrous and we can't be truly happy until we've raped, neutered and butchered her to death.

The tenet of his-story, to make division consistent and absolute, has found monsters wherever its gaze has lingered. There are monsters of other nations and monsters of different religions. Essentially anything different has been judged monstrous. At the time of European colonization, every newly discovered tribe seemed savage; its members – costumed or naked, decorated with bone, feather and paint, inked, pierced and most likely dancing – seemed to be, in the words of one contemporary onlooker, 'screaming and clapping their hands like so many demons'.

Now that the Earth has been connected and fully conquered, it is to space that we go to find our nightmares. The monster of *Alien* created by HR Giger was a masterstroke, combining multiple archetypes of our fear. It was a monster of many parts. The slimy egg opened to reveal a scuttling spider-like creature that would leap onto the face with muscular persistence, bind itself around the neck, lock its eight legs around the head and, in a parody of the romantic embrace, plant a fatal kiss to impregnate with its spore. Then the host was ruptured, guts exploding in an abysmal version of birth, with a small, penile baby mewling menacingly from the eviscerated murder-scene. The alien itself was a fantastic terror: disguising itself in shadows before either killing or snatching the body away and webbing it for later impregnation. The fact it had acid for blood and its only motive was mindless killing and procreation – the presence of the Queen with her long intestinal chute laying egg after egg (an endless breeding machine of the horror) – managed to unite in one form a hundred of our pathological fears of the natural world.

By using so many versions of human procreation, it painted an interesting picture of how we're repulsed by our own coming-into-being. The entombing of the web, a reminder of the way spiders catch and keep their prey alive until they're ready for them, was another grossness of Nature. And the laying of eggs by insects in their hundreds, depicting the process of feminine fertility, another reason for mankind to get out the chemicals and start spraying. In reducing the point of the alien to an eating, breeding and killing machine, it showed the disgust with which our rational mind views the necessities of life. To begin to deconstruct the film, to argue that for such an intelligent life to get around the universe would require technical skills, is to bring the alien back to earth: give it a tool shed and possibly a tune to whistle. But we don't want to humanize our monsters because to do so makes them more like us. Their methods of ensuring life become our own. Their ability to be single-minded to the point of genocide seems uncomfortably familiar.

It is humanity that has repeatedly shown itself to be monstrous. His-story is littered with the rule of men who have led armies, killed thousands and tortured more. But every mass-murderer, every Adolf Hitler or Muammar Gaddafi, seems to inspire only further cruelty rather than forgiveness. We are encouraged to find and kill any human monsters, unaware of the monstrosity of our own voices screaming, 'Kill!' I lived on Brick

Lane in London when a lone individual called David Copeland (whose own monsters included black, Asian and gay people) exploded nail bombs in Brixton, Soho and on my street. What struck me more than the nails was the response by a local when she decreed that Copeland 'Should be strung up with piano wire.' It seems that whatever race, creed or land we belong to, we are capable of producing our fair share of monsters. And the way we treat them – burning them at the stake, running them through with a sword, taking them out and shooting them – reveals far more about our own latent monsters than any external hideousness.

The modern monsters are the pedophile and the terrorist. At a festival recently the game du jour, among a handful of 9-year-olds, was avoiding being caught by the sex monster. The fear is growing that the monsters move among us. They walk beside us and look the same as us. Since 9/11, the constant warnings of terror have made threatening the most banal of objects: the water bottle, the shoe, the ominous rucksack. The theft of Madeleine McCann in 2007 fuelled the fear that *they* (the ordinary-looking ones) were coming for our children. And while the atomizing of society has promised protection from the 'big bad' with entry codes and individual keys, the absence of us as creatures of community means we don't trust anyone who may be outside the front door, however normal they may appear.

Still the monster lurks outside. What if the reality is something else, something akin to what William Golding wrote in *The Lord of the Flies* when Simon meets with the dead pig's head on a stick and gives it voice:

> 'Fancy thinking the Beast was something you could hunt and kill!' said the head. For a moment or two the forest and all the other dimly appreciated places echoed with the parody of laughter. 'You knew, didn't you? I'm part of you? Close, close, close! I'm the reason why it's no go? Why things are what they are?'

Despite the shadowy suspicion that something horrible haunts the island, it is the masculine champions among the boys who end up terrorizing and killing the others. The most monstrous actions are not perpetrated by aliens, animals, or any external fiends: they are the forces that lie dormant in every one of us.

Is it controversial to suppose that these great demons of our nightmares are not outside but inside us? After all, Dr. Jekyll was his own worst enemy. One of the inceptors of the Stanford Prison Experiment in 1971, Philip Zimbardo, wrote *The Lucifer Effect* to show how easily any one of us can become the brutal torturer, given certain conditions. Each of us has the potential, if we choose, to rob a house, steal a child or murder a family. To decrease the likelihood of doing so requires us first to accept this, and then to regularly, safely, expel the little monsters that lurk inside each of us. The most monstrous behavior can even arise in the name of love. The transition of Anakin Skywalker to Darth Vader comes because he cannot make peace with losing the one he loves. So if love can do that, is it surprising it can smack a child, rape a woman and bully a friend?

For the monsters we carry inside us to be released safely, we have to begin to look at how this can be achieved and listen to how other cultures have accomplished it. Might we need a safe space, like a circle, giving them costumes, a mask and voices; letting them be acted out in a way that expels them without aim at an individual or group? To shit and piss out what we don't need is one of the daily essentials of life. To be able to do the same with our emotional garbage (our fears, paranoia, anger and monstrous screaming) would go some way to reduce the quantity of daily horrors that broadcast into our homes. Perhaps this is one of the roles of dancing. Irrational it might seem to behave like the dancer whom 5 Rhythms® creator Gabrielle Roth observed as 'a snake-woman slithering into teenage boy, into grandmother, into panther, into eagle'. But maybe taking the form of other creatures is to give them a stage, to enact them through ritual, to release them in such a way that no one is hurt.

The experience of the American anthropologist Michael Harner may offer insight into why the existence of monsters haunts us. Following his consumption of the drug ayahuasca to partake in the shamanic method of journeying, he was shown giant reptilian creatures reposing sluggishly at the bottom of his brain. These creatures

> projected a visual scene in front of me … Black specks dropped from the sky by the hundreds and landed in front of me on the barren landscape. I could see the 'specks' were actually large, shiny, black creatures with stubby pterodactyl-like wings and huge whale-like bodies … The creatures then showed me how they had created life on the planet in order to hide within the multitudinous forms and thus disguise their presence … I learned that the dragon-like creatures were thus inside of all forms of life, including man. They were the true masters of humanity and the entire planet, they told me. We humans were but the receptacles and servants of these creatures.

Disturbed and exhilarated by being presented with such irrational illumination, Harner then went to seek out a local blind shaman, who had made many excursions into the spirit worlds, and told him of his encounter with the dragon-like creatures who claimed they were the true masters of the world. The response of the shaman? 'He stared up toward me with his sightless eyes, and said with a grin, "Oh, they're always saying that."'

FD Roosevelt said during the American Depression, 'The only thing we have to fear is fear itself.' In making a game of things that scare us, we perform the 'Ridikulus' spell that JK Rowling includes in *The Prisoner of Azkaban*; that of combating fear by laughing at it. If the horror lurks like a giant bat-whale-dragon creature inside everything, then there's one sitting in you while you're reading this. And if we can laugh at it (I imagine mine in a pink tutu performing arabesques) then we keep it small, belittling it. Recent films like *Shrek* and *Monsters Inc.* perform the same feat: taking the ogres and dragons of fairy tales and making them funny; daring to humanize them. They give back to the 'other' the very qualities that his-story has sought to make exclusive to the rational, white male. Not least the last laugh.

In shamanic teaching there is an upper and lower world, spiritual worlds we can access from the physical realm of Middle Earth for healing and guidance. The upper world is the place of spirit in human form (angels, gods, aliens, higher beings) and the lower world is the place of spirit in animal form (fish, insect, mammal, hybrid, chimera). Journeying to these worlds is safe because they are the realms of compassionate spirit, and without body there is no pain. It's only in the middle world of mortality where suffering can be experienced. It's here that spirit takes form, where we can be stung, bitten and knocked. It's here that we can lose ourselves, become obsessed, disappointed, enraged, and in the process, hurt ourselves and others. In finding ways to move beyond the mess we've inherited and now have the chance to consciously affect, we need to find methods to help ourselves heal. Instead of inflicting more suffering on those whose inner monsters have gone too far, whose suffering finds form in tyranny, abuse and murder, we could help all our little monsters to stay snoozing, or come out safely in pantomime and performance. Irrational it is: unscientific, definitely. But as the old maps of the sea used to show us, whether we like it or not: 'Here be monsters.'

Daring to Move

Dancing has had an interesting experience across the last 5,000 years. It has survived, despite increasingly brutal waves of hate, suggesting it's more than simply a chance to embarrass yourself to Whigfield, come 'Saturday Night'. Why should dancing be so controversial? Why should we have been made to fear getting into our bodies and busting a move? Why should the only permissible dance for hundreds of years, witnessed in any number of Jane Austen adaptations, be the sort that makes cardboard and clockwork out of our muscles? And why should people in authority repeatedly talk about dancing as the *devil's work*? What exactly is so dangerous about getting our groove on?

Would it surprise you to learn that it hasn't always been thus? Every tribal society performs dance rituals of some kind or another. As Mead observed in Samoa, 'Dancing is the only activity in which almost all ages and both sexes participate.' Then there's the tribe in Borneo that selects its new leader by holding a dancing competition – last one standing becomes the chief. Dancing offers a connection with the cosmos, mirroring the movement of the seasons, the waxing and waning of the moon. And the ecstatic dancing rituals of so many indigenous peoples often have healing as well as religious functions, if the two need to be distinguished. Social, inclusive, spiritual and healing, in cultures far removed from our own, dancing has been prized as nothing short of essential.

The centrality of dancing to the human experience can be seen from the records of western colonizers and missionaries who dropped anchor off distant lands and met with people who danced as a matter of course. But what is also clear is the sense of two disparate worldviews colliding. Contemporary reports from explorers, traders and missionaries abound with incomprehension. Among them was Charles Darwin, who was repelled by the *corroborree* rite of western Australians and judged the dance 'a most rude, barbarous scene ... without any sort of meaning'. Words used in relation to dancing include *depraved, hideous, grotesque* and *hellish.* As Barbara Ehrenreich comments in her book *Dancing in the Streets*, 'Trance was what many of those wild rituals seemed to lead up to, and for Europeans, it represented the very heart of darkness – a place beyond the human self.' Why should dancing, so central to other cultures, appear to the western tradition as *demonic*? Why should this apparent 'leaving of the self' cause such fear? Why were our ancestors strangers to the dance?

The answers lie once more in this story of his. Monotheism, as we have seen, emphasizes segregation, classification and division at the expense of uniting, joining and harmonizing. Again and again, dancing appeared to the masculine authorities as an example of the *evil* old way, of Goddess worship and of those in touch with the feminine arts of instinctive movement, both sexual and ecstatic. Despite the appearance of gods like Dionysus and Jesus (figures for whom dance and celebration were integral to life), the masculinized order of rule persistently and violently attacked dancing for the qualities of unity and togetherness it offered. It wasn't just that dancing represented the feminine. For a ruling body that sought control and hierarchical stability, dancing was dangerous. It upset the social order; making kings of fools and fools of kings.

To the Roman Empire, dancing was part of the cult of the Great Mother, Cybele, and the potential of it to unseat the dominant culture was never far away. For the church fathers of Christendom, the fact Jesus himself danced and encouraged dancing within churches was something to be played down. Dancing not only threatened the physical structure of churches, with potential damage to buildings and objects, but also threatened the psychic power of the priesthood. *Ecstasy* (a word derived from the Greek meaning 'to stand outside oneself'), gave people power. They were afforded direct personal communion with divinity through dance. If unchecked, they would have no need for the intervening rule of priests. Because dancing provides virtuosi but no formal teachers, affording equal value to everyone's dance, it must have been akin to revolution for a church that worked in parallel with feudalism by enforcing hierarchy and keeping everyone in their place.

Dancing was banned from churches in England in the 13th century, so the people congregated outside. Then dancing was banned from the surrounding area until, with the rise of Puritanism, dancing was forbidden altogether. The association between devilry and dancing can be seen in Arthur Miller's play *The Crucible*, concerning the Salem witch hunts of the 17th century. Missionaries declared dancing to be an example of devilry, and as western society became rationalized and secularized, dancing was judged *savage* and *mad*. The growth of secular political hierarchies meant anything that brought people together was feared as seditious. The establishment of aristocratic modes of behavior worthy of emulation meant silence and sedentary behavior were praised, and anything mobile and loud was looked down upon. Dancing became a problem of class and a problem of race, until finally it was condemned as a problem of youth. At every turn, the critique of thousands of years of masculine rule was heard: dancing was *bad*.

It was the Rock 'n' Roll rebellion of the 1950s that witnessed the beginning of the reclamation within western culture of the dance. The music was a link with African culture, containing common characteristics of African, African-American and much Caribbean music, such as polyrhythms, antiphonal responses, and a potential for both repetition and creative variation. Despite forced exile, slavery and prejudice, it was black culture that kept the dance alive by keeping the music going. Emerging first through jazz in the 1920s, it erupted after the Second World War through Bebop and Rock, and spread like jam. There was no division between hearing music and getting up to dance. A black plantation preacher wrote that the way his people had worshipped involved them singing, accompanied by an ecstasy of motion, clapping of hands and tossing of heads. Nothing like this had occurred in the context of Christian worship since dance was prohibited in European churches. And unlike the permitted aristocratic forms of movement, this new dance reeked of sexuality with the bump and grind of sweat-drenched bodies. Rapidly, uncontrollably, this participatory experience of dancing, rooted in an ecstatic spiritual tradition, was back and spreading among the so-called *secular* venues of dance halls.

In the early part of the 20th century, audience participation was reserved for military parades and fascist spectacles. Rock was different. It inspired people. It summoned them to the dance like the Pied Piper, and the dance evoked, in the words of writer Ray Pratt, 'the unleashing of generations of repressed sexuality', in much the same way that the death of Princess Diana in 1997 witnessed the outpouring of generations of repressed grief. Rock struck with such force in the fifties and sixties because the white world it entered was frozen over and brittle, physically and emotionally paralyzed. To the Black Panther leader Eldridge Cleaver, white rock fans were simply trying to reclaim their bodies after generations of disembodied existence. The anger at rock music from the authorities was as vivid as the dancing. Some clergymen raised the possibility that rock could turn young people into devil worshippers. Anti-rock commentary echoed the language that 18th- and 19th-century Europeans had used to denounce native ecstatic rituals. But something had been remembered. This time the dancing would not be stopped. Jazz, Rock, Soul, Blues, Motown, Reggae, Funk, Disco, House, Garage, R and B, Hip Hop, DubStep: all these black-inspired musical genres have filtered out of the underground and into everyone's daily experience. Much is owed to those who kept the sacred rhythms alive.

Despite the attempts of successive waves of church leaders and politicians, the beat goes on. From the first all-night party at Alexandra Palace in 1967 onwards, the UK has witnessed its own revolution in dancing. We are shaking our thang again on a scale unwitnessed for millennia, and it is no coincidence that the biggest chemical drug to facilitate this collective movement is named after the very experience dancing enables: Ecstasy.

In his book *Altered States*, Matthew Collins documents the story of 'Ecstasy Culture', which he called 'the combination of dance music (in all its many and various forms) and drugs'. Ecstasy and House music leaked across the seas from Ibiza and Chicago around 1987 and did nothing less than rouse millions of people to the dance floor. It was the most successful way to deliver altered states of consciousness. As Sadie Plant says in *Writing on Drugs*, it was dance music's repetitive beats that 'had little to do with the representations and accompaniments of song. This was music as a matter of modifying state of mind … music that remembered the techniques of dance and drumming, rhythm, trance'.

Those who understood the market possibilities of such a triumphant 'entertainment format' might have milked it, but the explosion of ecstasy in this island has changed the way people feel, act and live. The benefit of altering states of consciousness is the depths they add to our experiences of the world. The potency of dancing as a social and healing activity has survived among those who no longer want or need to take drugs; while those born years after the Second Summer of Love continue to embrace the mix of sound, light, people and costumes.

In Robin Sylvan's work on the spiritual transformation within dance, one raver observed how people involved with the dance scene are evolving: 'You can see it in the individuals in the community … they are growing, they're becoming stronger … they have an interest in the workings of the world and are willing and interested in impacting it in positive ways.' Dancing is not a means of escaping the body, but a way to let the body escape the structures and boundaries that ordinarily keep it organized. It opens up a space where the unknown past and the emergent future meet and, contrary to thousands of years of directives, provides a culture with options in place of rules. The 1994 Criminal Justice and Public Order Bill was the work of a government so threatened by the successful rise in raves and free parties that it banned unlicensed gatherings of more than ten people, who had come together to listen to music, in the words of the Act, 'wholly or predominantly characterized by the emission of a succession of repetitive beats'. Even this didn't stop the dancing, but the need for people to get a license and charge an entry fee has co-opted dancing into an enterprise of capital. Dancing in its pure form is a birthright to all of us (like feasting, play and creativity) and requires neither cash card nor chemical tablet industry.

Dancing presents great challenges to the social hierarchy. The resilience of differing but similar power bodies in wanting to shut off the music has been impressive, if counterproductive. To generate societies deprived of innate avenues for collective joy only worsens the social predicament. Those in positions of authority become more fearful of the crazy mob, while ordinary people face the deleterious effects of continued disempowerment. Following colonialism, many indigenous cultures were forbidden to dance. The peoples of Tahiti saw Protestantism as 'dour and cheerless' as a result, and among the Namaquas of South Africa it was said that someone who converted to Christianity had 'given up dancing'. Unlike the paranoia that dancing necessitates drug abuse and addiction, it seems the reverse is true. Without the opportunity to dance, many indigenous people turned to alcoholism and despair. The lie of materialism becomes another self-defeating dependency as people amass more and more objects in the hope of purchasing a happiness that can be achieved simply by dancing. Without collective dancing there is lethargy, depression, obesity, inertia, isolation, and an overriding feeling of poverty.

It is no coincidence that following the arrival of Ecstasy and dance culture, people's experiences of spiritual communion increased. Unlike the ordered church service, dance culture has opened people to the divinity within them. As Sylvan says, 'Ravers typically do not perform these dance movements because they are aesthetically pleasing to watch from the outside, but because they produce powerful somatic states experienced from the inside.' A metaphor commonly voiced among dancers, and that traditionally expresses the idea of access to spirits and spiritual worlds, is that of a vertical connection that begins in the earth and touches the divine realm as it reaches upwards. This is an image that goes all the way back to shamanism and the Axis Mundi (world center); congruent with the ideas of Kundalini Yoga and of energy waking up to levels of spiritual relation, as sap rises from below.

It isn't surprising that many dancers think of their clubs, as the Faithless song 'God is a DJ' puts it, as their 'church … where I heal my hurts'. It is not a crime to yearn for a connection with the sacred, but many of the religious institutions that were supposed to provide us with this connection perpetuate divisions that are at the root of our contemporary crises. Rather than try to force the differences to be unified, music empowers us to come together. This would seem to be one of the reasons why dancing has been so central to those cultures that didn't suffer the same institutionalized imbalance. The feminine music seduces and entices us; we are willing participants of the dance and, without force, happily surrender to a unity without any aggrieving lack of choice or disempowerment. So it is that Sufis speak of dancing as 'an auxiliary means of spiritual concentration', and indigenous people around the Amazon undertook dancing as well as other sacred rituals in the effort 'to be more than *one* self'. In the contemporary dance scene, ravers speak of how the powerful peak-experiences on the dance floor break down traditional boundaries of race, class, sexual orientation and gender; bringing everyone together in an ecstatic unity that transcends difference. It is ironic that the desire for unity, made crazed within our culture through violence and bloodshed, is effortless when left to the beat of the drum.

That dancing is fun can be attested by anyone with personal experience of it. That dancing can have physical benefits seems obvious, even to gym instructors. But dancing is also the tool of a circular sense of life, and forges community. Dancing brings people together and offers an opportunity to release the ideological restraints of the created self. Through dance you can lose yourself, becoming one within the group and part of the infinite landscape. Dancing dissolves dualities. It turns opposites into complements and can bring profound healing at the personal and group level. Dancing helps us to move deeper into our bodies and empty our minds, making it possible for spirit to enter us to effect healing. The ecstatic state cannot be controlled by another. It cannot be dispatched or restricted. It is wild and glorious and senseless, and all the better for it.

Gabrielle Roth paid attention to the underlying rhythmical movements of tribal dance and developed the wave of 5 Rhythms®. The widening popularity of the form has in turn led to other dance groups that honor the circle of communal experience and the equality of all dancers under a drum. The tenet of 5 Rhythms® is analogous to life; the dance moves from the feminine Flow to the masculine Staccato, then into the alchemical possibilities of harnessing the two in Chaos. Following this is the elevated and emptied Lyrical state before the wave closes in Stillness. Moving away from any association between dance and drugs, the wave of the rhythms encourages a spiritual connection through music, movement and community. There is no age limit, people dance barefoot, and within the dance are the possibilities of trance, spiritual ecstasy and divine personal connection. The only requirement is to move. As Roth says, 'This is soul retrieval, something we all need to do in order to heal an ancient and universal wound ... Disempowerment is our major wound. This divorce of spirit from flesh, masculine from feminine, light from dark, is the loss of the soul.'

The popularity from the 1980s onwards of musical theater in London's West End provoked outrage from advocates of *serious* theater. But the kind of musical experience has itself changed. Modern successes like *Mamma Mia* (whose storyline of matrilineal inheritance over that of patrilineal is another example of the returning feminine) and the anti-apartheid *Hairspray* encourage the audience to stir from their seats: inciting them to scream, cheer, sing and dance along with the performance. Whether at gigs, festivals, concerts, raves and now even theater, we are finding our feet and becoming part of the performance, regaining perhaps a sense that such expressions of music and dancing are meant to be participatory, to be shared between all of us.

Another development over the last 40 years is the proliferation of festivals, among which Glastonbury is a potent example. Not only in the dance, but queuing for food, offering healing and practicing crafts, people are coming together. They are doing so in communities, celebrating life in diversity, remembering themselves as creatures of body living with the body of the land. The excessive materialism of the departing culture still demands tickets, camping equipment and the semiotic minefield of flip flop brands, but the concept of direct personal experience (off-grid, in the wild, round fires and under stars) suggests we are remembering the untapped spiritual wealth of greater simplicity. For many people, festivals remind them of the possibilities of barter; free tickets for stewarding, clothing swapped for massage, food in place of washing up.

Perhaps the greatest symbol of dancing is what it says about our willingness to move. Each step to the beat is a step towards empowerment; each personal revelation is an encouragement to share and be heard. Unlike armies there is no conscription, and with only the music calling to us, there is neither argument nor reason. There is just the drum, the voice, the rhythm and the melodies: speaking to us directly, inspiring us to return to a world of joy, singing us back. If the more we dance, the better we feel, this is something the whole world needs more than ever. It's not just about entertainment or egotistic self-indulgence, but massive global healing. As Kylie reminded us at the start of this millennium: 'Your Disco Needs You!'

Healing Circle

How are you? It's one of the most common questions we ask each other when we meet, and typically requires a clipped response. Anything too protracted seems self-indulgent. We're all fine really, aren't we? We're getting by, as Amy Sedaris prescribed, 'accentuating the positives and medicating the negatives'.

If the extent of that self-medication with both legal and illegal drugs is anything to go by, we're not doing well at all. The global trade in illegal drugs is second only to the legal traffic of armaments. The volume of alcohol consumed is staggering, with many city streets given over to socially sanctioned alcoholism each weekend. Tablets are now the most common method of conventional medicine, and even the complementary market is saturated with nutritional supplements. We might have a longer life expectancy, but the quality of that life seems far lower than the one sold to us through adverts. Stress is an omnipresent complaint. Fatigue, inertia, anxiety, panic and depression are accommodated as necessary side effects for our so-called comfortable life. Hospitals are incubators for disease. Positive health seems rare, and the specter of a vast contagion, such as SARS, winging a lift on global air traffic feels frighteningly overdue.

The sickness of our bodies is congruent with the way we treat them. We've seen how his-story has separated mind from body. The more self-consciousness has grown, the more alien seem the vessels that give our brains mobility and support. The logic of division has promoted surgery, with operations on specific parts of the body being favored over any long-term consideration of the well-being of the individual as a whole. The promise of surgery to remove cancers is matched by the ability of the cancers to recur, with the surgery itself prompting the growth of abnormal cells through physical violation. While western medicine offers unarguably successful operations, it doesn't entertain the question of how far our way of living causes these diseases in the first place. Combined with the range of reports concerning the inefficacy of tablets and their crippling side effects, conventional medicine seems as far from the Hippocratic oath ('Do nothing that harms the patient') as you can get.

Having detailed how disharmony has pervaded this 5,000-year period, it should come as no surprise that we are sick as a result. Health, like riding a bicycle, is all about balance. Even as far back as the start of this age, we find the seeds of long-term sickness being sown. Diseases increased through the development of cities, with farmers living among their own sewage providing microbes with a short path from one person's body to another's drinking water. The Black Death of 1348 decimated the cities where people lived in close contact, sharing the same contaminated resources and breathing the same air. When the early colonists traveled to America, it was with diseases both accidental and intentional: attacking the unity of the indigenous societies and passing them smallpox-infested blankets.

With concerted effort, the people who could have provided help and healing were penalized and extinguished. As Matilda Joslyn Gage wrote in her 19th-century work *Woman, Church and State*, 'The superior learning of witches was recognized in the widely extended belief of their ability to work miracles.' As knowledge is power, the church feared women having healing abilities and leveled its deadliest blows at them. These wise women healers, who maintained the traditions of prehistory as spread from mouth to ear, had learned the virtues and uses of herbs. Yet, as Gage continues, 'an acquaintance with herbs soothing to pain, or healing in their qualities, was then looked upon as having been acquired through diabolical agency'. In their work on *Witches, Midwives and Nurses*, Barbara Ehrenreich and Deidre English note that this suppression coincided with the creation of a new male medical profession. Like the priesthood, who outlawed women practicing healing, the new medical establishment needed to discredit other practices to ensure its own success. Chemistry became superior to alchemy, medicine superior to mystery, and masculine science provably better than old wives' tales. The Doctor became a highly respected, powerful (and male) figure, whose principles of supreme knowledge and diagnosis, prescription and proscription, you doubted at your peril.

With such sustained and reasoned imbalance our world got sicker until it became affected by what Mary Daly calls 'iatrogenic illness', an 'epidemic of doctor-made disease'. In buying the masculine cure, we, as individuals and a world, have become more ill. The imbalance of this age is written into the prescription for its cure. The idea of finding our succor in Nature is dismissed by western medicine, as is the concept that each of us could be powerful enough to develop means of healing ourselves and each other. Stemming from the theory that the world is unsatisfactory and can only become perfect through the busy interference of the masculine, we are witnessing a world that is sickening further with every dose of medicine she is force-fed. The familiar chorus of the doctor ('It's for your own good') sounds increasingly sinister when evidently resulting in so many personal and global symptoms of disease.

As we've seen, the plight of the honeybee demonstrates the problem of trying to mend something while still insisting that it work at punishing rates. Like those of the bees, our immune systems are dangerously compromised by over-work, stress, pesticides and chemicals. Yet we too are forbidden from unplugging ourselves to rest and recuperate in our own time, furnished with more drugs to numb us into continued exertion. It's a logic whose limits are shown by the effects on bacteria and insects by ever more complex chemicals. Resistance to streptomycin, the original TB drug, was first reported in 1948. Since then, the bacillus has also bred resistance to rifampicin and isoniazid as well as to many second-line oral antibiotics and third-line injectable drugs. As a result, XDR-TB (extremely drug resistant) is a strain now classed by the World Health Organization as 'virtually untreatable'. We know that new insect generations arise in a matter of days and weeks, for which the answer can't be more insecticides. Yet the scientific and conventional health bodies have concurred that better insecticides are exactly what are needed, for which genetic modification has been invented.

As the chemicals increase, so do the number of cases of people reporting ill-health. In 1984, as a neighboring farm began crop spraying, Georgina Downs developed flu-type symptoms, a blistered sore throat and headaches. Seven years later she was hospitalized with severe muscle wastage and muscle weakness as a direct result of the chemicals sprayed onto crops and into the ground. The horrors of inherited mutations, abnormalities and deformities, visited upon the people of Vietnam by the American bombardment of Agent Orange and Napalm onto their land and into their water supply, remain current. With evidence of adverse reactions to chemicals and surgery multiplying daily, must we continue to hear those to whom we've bequeathed our power saying, 'Up the dose'? What choice do we have? How else can we get better?

The last century has seen a resurgence in complementary therapies. From Indian practices like yoga, to traditional Chinese acupuncture, the western world is waking up to find there are other ways to keep mind-body-spirit in harmony than reasoning with the mind, cutting open the body, and removing the spirit. Though they can wear relatively recent costumes (such as Reiki discoverer Dr Usui in late 19th-century Japan and reflexology foot-mapper Eunice Ingham in 1930s America), the roots of hands-on healing go back to ancient times. Evidence of reflexology has been found in Egyptian hieroglyphs, and the prevalence of hands-on healing within indigenous cultures can be seen in the way every part of the globe has its own version of massage. Like a 'to-do' list from *Absolutely Fabulous*, we can now choose between homeopathy, shiatsu, crystal healing, naturopathy and rebirthing. What re-emerged as an alternative to the rule of doctors has grown in credibility and popularity. More and more of us are seeking answers in complementary therapies when western medicine fails us, or when we lose faith in its premise.

Many within conventional medicine criticize these therapies for being unscientific. Holistic therapies aren't scientific because their theoretical base is completely different from the base on which science is founded. Rather than see only the physical body, holism asks us to consider our emotional, mental and spiritual bodies too. Rather than treat the symptom, holistic therapists look for the cause, and rather than treat the disease they treat the patient. Holism also encourages us to take matters into our own hands, rather than becoming dependent on doctors and drugs. It recommends that we, for instance, meditate, practice altering our destructive mindsets, and change the situation that is dis-easing us. For people who train in and use complementary healing, they are their first clients, becoming well in themselves before affirming the strength to work with others and engaging in swaps with other practitioners to ensure the maintenance of good health. It might seem a luxury to those in the rush of modern society, but then we have to ask ourselves: how important is it to rush further into sickness?

For western science, it's a challenge to open up to concepts like the subtle energy body and spiritual health, because nowhere in science's dictionary is subtle energy and soul given credence. The non-physicality of the soul was taken by a materialist system as proof of its non-existence. Therefore it is challenging for many western medics to hear phrases such as 'soul loss' or 'intrusions at an energetic level'. According to the rubric of *conventional* medicine, they fear they are straying into the world of mental illness. But shamanic practitioners across the world not only accept terms like psychic surgery, soul retrieval and extraction; they have worked with their spirit allies to help those afflicted for tens of thousands of years. Working on the spirit level works with the root of problems that, unchecked, manifest on the physical. According to shamanism, if we experience trauma, parts of our soul will separate to ensure we continue to live. If these parts aren't retrieved we walk around with holes inside us which are wide-open to negative intrusions, repressed emotions, and self-destructive thoughts and actions. If nothing is done about these then they can manifest as increasingly severe physical ailments. The survival of terms like *prahna* and *chi*, together with, one could almost say, scientific, theories of energy movement such as meridians and chakras, suggests that though talk of energetic health was chased underground, it did not vanish. And its continuing revival provides the surest hope that more of us are committing to take healing back into our own hands.

It is little wonder that the British Medical Association, long-studying doctors-to-be and pharmacists are threatened by every Jane, Joe and Aunt Flo discovering they too have the personal power to effect healing; able to give their time, love and energy to those in need. Holism listens to the life and practices of the individual, engages simply with human touch, and encourages deep relaxation, communication and daily practice. Problematically, for laboratory-based scientism, holism cannot be taken away from the world, broken up and blind tested. Those who work holistically are humble enough to know that the treatment comes through them not from them and that Nature herself (in the form of rest, exercise, a nutritional diet, plenty of fresh air and water) is the best means to good health. Corporate medicine balks at these remedies, not just because they come from those outside the closed shop of the professional medical establishment, but because they cost nothing. From the perspective of a global pharmaceutical industry worth around

£300 billion, going for a nice walk won't increase their profits. Greed, whether coming from pharmaceutical companies or those equally materially-minded celebrity gurus trying to push their trademarked and personality-drenched supplements at exorbitant prices, finds less profit in helping people get well than in keeping them hungering for health.

For scientism, critical and panicky about loss of power over others, as well as loss of profit, one of the arguments against complementary medicine is that it is just faith healing. Any improvement among people having homeopathy or crystal healing rests on the placebo effect; the power of the mind to believe itself back to good health. It's a criticism that has become more vocal, the more fundamental the global climate grows. One of the leading interrogators of complementary medicine is Ben Goldacre, whose book *Bad Science* is the extension of his work as a columnist for the *Guardian*. But even Goldacre marvels when faced with the placebo effect. It's not just that the placebo effect exists; it's that it can be repeatedly shown to be beneficial at minimal cost and without intrusive surgery. Take the acupuncture test, which tested people who suffered chronic back pain: 27% found relief just by being part of a medical test; 47% were relieved by having needles stuck into them according to traditional acupuncture; and 44% felt better by having 'a bloke sticking pins anywhere'. The results show not only that acupuncture can be effective, but that even people working by instinct alone can prove beneficial when possessing ritual and theater and when people expect it to work. Or take the hotel cleaners, split into two groups. One group was told how much exercise they were getting and the others were left alone. The group who had been tutored perceived they did more exercise and, despite no change in actual exercise levels, demonstrated a significant change for the better in every single one of the health measurements recorded.

Placebos work not because a sugar pill has power, but because we are amazing creatures. We can choose to believe things and make them real (literally, making things matter). We can think ourselves into illness and think ourselves well. This says much about our personal abilities to change the health of our bodies when we choose to, by how we think and behave, and comes closer to finding an explanation for the resilient phenomenon of miracles and miraculous healing. This is not a second best, but an intriguing insight into the power of our mind to effect changes in our body and to connect with the healing resources of the multiverse.

And while miraculous healing does occur, one of the most profound experiences for us as individuals and healers is to remember humility and to stand witness to the inevitability of Death. As Helen Garner wrote in her recent novel *The Spare Room*, 'Death will not be denied. To try is grandiose. It drives madness into the soul. It leaches out virtue. It injects poison into friendship and makes a mockery of love.' We all have to die, and sometimes the most successful healer is the one who readies the person for death, for making the transition from this world to the next.

We can affect our bodies, our environment and each other in ways that we are only now beginning to consciously remember. We can make this world a paradise or a hell. As we return to coming together in circle, let's remember the magnified power of group healing to help an individual, so their dis-ease lessens and they can more quickly resume their place as vital and active members of the community. Practices like meditation reduce the internal anxiety that can worry a slight discomfort into a terrible illness. Tablets owe their active ingredients to plants and plant wisdom. But whereas tablets attempt to better them, they lack the complex synergy of ingredients found in plants. And of course plants, like kind touch and exercise, are free. Increasingly we find our healing where we left it: quietly, ordinarily, miraculously, growing as a weed by the hedge. And if such remedies are available within and around us, unmediated by fee-charging, over-burdened professionals, helped by our practices and supported by feeling at home in the world, then maybe we have the chance to move out of anxieties over ill-health. Maybe we could actually become well.

Magical Thinking

Children get the possibilities of magical transformation in the world as easily as they find ways to play. No one needs to be taught fun, though prolonged battering, condemnation and criticism can make the land of make-believe seem unreachable. To 'make-believe' is one of the core requirements of play. The bed sheet becomes a gown, the old box a crown; dolls converse and rocks speak. And it takes a guardian of bitter experience to instruct a child that, in reality, frogs do not become princes.

Artists, writers and musicians persist in the belief that gold can be fashioned from lead, that a piece of tubing can play a tune, and a lump of clay can become a beautiful figure. But for many grown-ups, the transition into adulthood becomes about putting away childish things. Money has become the only transformative power we believe in, magicking homes, food and holidays into existence. The parenting of children seems to have an unwritten clause that imagination only lasts until school tests get SAT.

But what if something very serious about play has been missed? What if these childish things are of the greatest value to us as creatures of sentience and soul? What if, by obliterating the ability, present in the circle, for things to be both one thing and the other, we have cauterized a crucial talent necessary for us to live well in the world?

At the time of the Protestant Reformation in the 16th century, much was made of the need to break the shackles of superstition. Idols and relics were all broken and burnt to make way for a more prosaic service, where the word was just the word. Among the theological quibbles lay the issue of transubstantiation that formed the meal of the catholic mass. The bread and wine, when consumed, were believed to actually transform into the body and blood of Christ. This was considered by the agents of reform to be ridiculous. At best, the new wave decreed, the bread and wine could 'symbolize' body and blood, but it was absurd to imagine they transformed. Wasn't it?

Our ancestors all over the world believed it wasn't absurd but essential. Australian Aborigines experience the sacred realm of Dreamtime as far more real than the material world. And within the UK our Celtic ancestors saw dreams as equally powerful as reality, helping to regenerate and re-orientate mind and body. But wherever the colonizing and missionary powers of Northern Europe went, they demonstrated the irrefutable power of the physical against the spiritual. They arrived on distant shores bringing the germs of new thinking. Physical diseases, alien to harmonious cultures, wiped out the shamans first and whole tribes soon after. Those who resisted faced the ideological germ of Christianity, which argued away their many gods and their native ways (including widespread animism, magical ritual and dancing), replacing them with the work ethic. Those who resisted still further met with the final germ of western power: the gun. The old way of balance between physical and spiritual was wiped out. That the spiritual could be crushed so easily by the physical was another weight to the argument that the dominating powers had might, as well as right, on their side.

The old way thought differently about objects and ideas. The power of something rested in the agreed understanding that it could transform. Like the body and blood of Christ, ancient cultures believed all life displayed a similar capacity for transformation. A tree was a physical life form with roots and leaves, but it was at the same time a divine being, a powerful aspect of spirit with powers of regeneration. The symmetry of roots and branches showed the reflection of the world: as above, so below. Macaw rituals in Meso-America managed to be both spiritual and practical at once, being both esoteric incantations and dances as well as methods of communicating practical significance. Every animal was respected as a form of god and spirit, each with its lessons to teach and power to honor, and when needed, borrow. Ancient cultures had no need for pets, because their entire ecosystem was a panoply of companionable life, both physical and divine. Furthermore, the harmony of this understanding, that trees and animals each needed and helped each other, required neither a scientific knowledge of carbon dioxide, nor the feverish anxiety over reducing its levels, because to live well in the world was to live in balance.

The act of transformation could be witnessed again and again, in dancing and ritual, where people moved outside themselves to make way for spiritual beings to enter. The placing of a mask on the head effected the transformation of the wearer into a god, for the sharing of the gifts of wisdom and healing. The mask was both a piece of carved wood and the gateway for the god. To see it as grossly physical and non-magical was to limit it, denying people inordinate power, health and learning. It was also to unbalance the way of the world, seeing it as restricted to one realm, instead of more. It also made it less fun.

Every act of theater is an act of transformation, and we register our confidence in an actor by their ability to morph before our eyes and become something other. The same can be said of shamans, who, under voluntary possession, offer Spirit a chance to make the invisible visible by coming into body. To see theater as superficial entertainment is to build up a Hollywood instead of a Holy Wood. In the absence of any other gods, we have had to make gods of our actors, ignoring the possibility of both magic and spirit, denying ourselves the miraculous. The cynicism with which this age has persistently viewed magic, preferring to see it as tricks, reflects our own sense of the world; not as something spectacular and humbling, but as something out to snare the unwary; to be belittled, dismantled and explained away.

When cinema first arrived in the 1920s, the silver screen must have breathed back a sense of the mythic. Giant faces, portraying the human experience in theaters across the western world, gave audiences a taste of what had, during his-story, been limited under religion and removed completely by science. We need our gods, and Hollywood cynically turned our appetite for them into a multi-billion-dollar industry. But our celluloid gods are mere mortals. They are fixed in film and destined to repeat the same lines over again. They are hounded by our cry for them, disrespected by a frenzy of flashbulbs, driven to drugs and madness or worse, into a collusion with the all-too-human industry that reminds them their power can only be expressed in the physical terms of Tiffany diamonds and Lear jets. Their egos are either smashed like the bodies they drive off the road, or inflated until they assume the error of hubris: of believing their soulless divinities to be greater than the divine.

With our desire for the mythic unceasing, we have turned, like Andy Warhol's factory, to anything physical we could worship: soup cans, hand bags, porn stars and pop acts, hoping that by worshipping them enough they might fully ascend and not fall. Their inability to do so has kept the wheel of celebrity turning, until, like auditions for reality shows, the queues of hopeful contestants stretch around the block.

The irony is that such transformation is possible for every one of us, if only we allow ourselves the humility to believe such immortal spirit comes through us; that when the mask is removed, so is the god, and we return to the small tasks of living ordinary lives; tending the garden, taking care of the old and feeding the fire. The power of transformation rests in coming back to earth, changing from the spectacular to the commonplace, recognizing that even after eating body and blood of the divine, we are still required by our humble mortality to shit and piss it out (itself an example of the ordinary miracle of transformation winding its way through the world).

The gross materialism of our age has led to billions of doors, without a sense of wonder at how transformative is the act of passing through any one of them. We seldom pause in the act of eating to consider what we are consuming or what power of transformation it has. We construct ever more complex toys, decked in the verisimilitude of 4-wheel-drive SUV or fridge-freezer, battery powered for illumination and movement, and seem baffled why our children find the infinite possibilities of the cardboard box more successful.

Modern art has been at the forefront of tempting us back to the baffling. In 1928 the Surrealist René Magritte painted a pipe and subtitled it *Ceci n'est pas une pipe* ('This is not a pipe'). In this and other works he was challenging our acceptance of the world of surfaces and the dogged belief that objects cannot embrace the impossible and be both one thing and another. From the 1970s, Conceptualist Michael Craig-Martin displayed a glass of water on a shelf and wrote an accompanying interview with himself explaining how it was in fact an oak tree. Craig-Martin asked himself whether intention causes the change and replied, 'I would say rather intention precipitates the change.'

The recent successes of *Harry Potter, The Lord of the Rings* and *His Dark Materials* show a willingness on the part of children of all ages to embrace the possibilities of magical transformation. There may be witches, angels and polar bears that can talk, after all. Our souls may well take on the form of an animal and be our most trusted ally. Despite the formula of the private school, JK Rowling's massive success in creating a magical world with familiar emotional complexities, more enticing than that of the lumbering Muggles, suggests we are eager to welcome the inexplicable back into our lives. That her books contain powerful spells disguised as readable narrative, only confirms the potential with magic to make the ordinary extra.

Ironically it is science that has, through rigorous logic, offered up suggestions that appear nothing short of irrational. The persistence of adaptation and evolution makes a mockery of attempts at classification. Psychoanalysis has shown the potential for magical transformation at a personal level, with successive schools of thought exploring how mindsets and patterns of behavior can alter. In the 1930s, searching for the equation that would explain everything, the closest Werner Heisenberg came was finding the equation to prove that you could never explain everything. The Mandelbrot Set offered a complement to pure geometry in the form of chaos theory, which showed Nature had a pattern for imperfect self-similarity that went further back than could be traced and would continue beyond into a future that couldn't be seen. And Quantum physics, revealing the interconnectedness of the atom under observation with the apparatus doing the observing, showed the limitation of objectivity and reminded us that we're all a part of this; paradoxically separate yet connected. Mystery has become so inherent in research that the exact sciences increasingly agree rationalism is not enough. Quantum now gives us films like *What the Bleep Do We Know?* and books like *The Tao of Physics* and *Meeting the Universe Halfway*, whereby the possibilities of the world become less rigid, more fuzzy and, if less certain, a lot more exciting. However large the particle-collider, it seems the order never catches up with the oddness.

At every level we are being presented with paradox. When we hunt less, we can find more. If we believe first, then we shall see. It is not rational: play, dance, games, music, theater, ritual and adventure never need a reason. And, paradoxically, the reason we do all of the above, celebrate them for children and adults alike, might be because they are as necessary to our well-being as that glass of water on the shelf, caught on its journey from drop to vapor, and in some cases, being an oak tree. Fun and games are not peripheral to our well-being; they are central. Perhaps the time has come for us to admit that life is poorer without the magic.

Traveling without Moving

Most people agree there's fun to be had going somewhere else and coming back again. Travel broadens the mind, opens the shutters and tans the body. New horizons, new tastes: we take some pictures and maybe pick up a souvenir. Much of our recent global culture has been shaped by the taste for travel, to the extent that mass movement of individuals is no longer a treat but a pattern and, in some cases, a commute. From land, to sea, to air, the desire to 'get away from it all' has become essential.

It's odd that civilizations so committed to settling into sedentary urban communities would make the desertion of such places a core part of their form. Outside his-story, wandering away and coming back happened differently. On the spiritual level, people would journey to spirit worlds, travel into the dimension of myth and imagination, without moving from their seat. On the physical level, the whole tribe moved around, following migrating animals and changing seasons and making the most of the variety of the planet. For tribes like the Sanema in the Orinoco Basin, nomadic hunting life took them where the animals were. They had no need for 'hunt-free zones' because when the levels of prey diminished they moved their whole village. The world was all yours, delineated into ancestral song-lines or represented by totem animals, but there was no sense of going home, because you never left. Everywhere you went was your home, and like a hermit crab, what was necessary came with you. Moving as a group meant you went at the pace of the slowest, which also gave people a lightness and sense of belonging. You didn't accumulate because you didn't want to be burdened, and wherever you went there was plenty. Everywhere, though different, made you feel welcome.

We've seen how settling into agricultural units was an act of fear that increased disease and made things separate. There was one part of the land for us and all other parts were not. So the degree of confidence at being at home became localized to the bit of earth with our fence round it. We became anxious about what we had. Was there enough? What if the harvest was bad? We were keen to increase our family to work the land more efficiently, and became antsy that other people would take away what we had. As the agricultural trend spread, so examples of individual success and wealth were paraded as what it was possible to achieve. Envy was encouraged and people made it their goal to get more and more at the expense of whatever stood in their way.

And so work began. Not a fulfilling habit of craft and purpose, but the hard work of doing well enough to be a success over other people; to get rich enough to have other people do the graft instead. Thus it seems that one of the signs that we were doing well from our appropriated plot of land was our ability to sign ourselves off and leave it.

To the mass of workers who became yoked to an area of land, the sight of their lords departing must have occasioned yet more envy. The rich had it all and they could leave it. Though this too became fraught with difficulties, namely robbers, the poor and desperate, waiting to hold up your caravan and steal your jewelry. So it became necessary to make sure you had secure homes en route – preferably the castles of other robber barons. In time, the need for faster transport and further distance was recognized. Nothing reduced the chances of being robbed at gunpoint than being able to travel faster than the robber (ideally leaving the ground altogether). As soon as the penniless plebs caught up with you, it was time to go further. Carriages, boats, steam engine, motor engine, jet engine … every means of transportation invented during this age has been available, first to the few who could afford it, who then required something more exclusive by the time the world and its limp caught up with them. Now that cars are everywhere, millions take cruises and air travel is nothing special, the rich let their next target appear beyond the stratosphere of the planet, with moon tours and space planes.

The mass of us stepping up to claim our slice of the reward for being obedient productive units means that the impact of travel has exploded. Most of the coast of southern and eastern Spain was long ago crowned with the proof of this in concrete. For somewhere else to be discovered means it won't be long before the place becomes a parody of itself: all neon lager signs and plastic snow globes. Across the world, the success of global capitalism has given body to the original idea of early settlers: that the signifier of how well you're doing in this world is how often you can get away from it. Whether taking the train to work in London, flying off to Italy every other weekend, or taking a year out to see the world, we seem to need continual motion to be able to stand our confinement. And because the requirements of travel grow ever more complex, with traffic jams, delays and breakdowns, time spent traveling can easily match the amount of time apportioned to being there.

The unforeseen irony of this desperate wanderlust is the homogeneity that results. We think we would like to see tribal Bhutan, but the hidden cost of reaching the most far-flung places is finding life almost exactly as we left it: the cans of coke, the cans of petrol, those endemic golden arches. It seems we can now go anywhere in the world, as long as we eat McDonald's. This is a relief for some travelers. The world looks familiar and local customs don't have to be engaged with. Whatever the dialect, there's a TV in the bedroom playing MTV and CNN, and the language of money is constant. The rise of global capitalism makes petrol stations, pollution hazes and wastelands phenomena in any language. If, as a Sioux proverb goes, 'we shall be known forever by the tracks we leave behind', we must ask what this pile-up of wasteful movement says about us.

Perhaps the most driving reason to get away from it all is the hope that travel will work its magic and change our lives. If we get to our island in the sun then anxieties will disappear and we will find happiness. It's a theme Alain de Botton explores in *The Art of Travel*, where the author indulges in a glorious fantasy of traveling to a tropical island, only to find the reality so much more crowded and banal. 'A momentous but until then overlooked fact was making itself apparent: I had inadvertently brought myself with me to the island.' So much of what we are sold as travel is the ruse that we will wake up on foreign shores and find ourselves different. But overspending in Manhattan is overspending in Bluewater; lack of fulfillment in Cheam is lack of fulfillment in New Zealand. We may hope that a train-ride or air flight will magic us into different people, but more often than not we find our habits enduring and our specters as mobile as we are.

There is much to be said for philanthropy. For increasing numbers of westerners their world trips are fueled by noble aims to end poverty, provide fresh water, save the world. But it remains the saddest irony that in buying into mass transportation and supporting the system of ownership and greed, we worsen the experiences of those people we had hoped to help. Bruce Parry's introduction to the Matis tribe in the Amazon revealed the cost of meeting the neighbors:

> Although their first official contact had been entirely peaceful – an exploratory visit by Brazil's National Foundation for Indians (FUNIA) – it had brought disaster in its wake, as they had subsequently mixed with loggers and miners working in the area and had contracted a number of western diseases. Within a few years epidemics had wiped out almost a third of their population.

Our dis-ease at enjoying what we have within ourselves, on our doorsteps, in our communities, has catapulted us far and wide, spreading the same dis-ease of disaffection and material aspiration wherever we land. This is the pattern every model of civilization has spread throughout his-story: a discontent with Nature, leading to a profusion of change (rapid novelty and exhaustion) that proves far more alienating, wasteful and polluting than what existed before. To a contemporary tribe member in Kombai in West Papua, ignorant of traveling capitalism, his encounter with its representative (Parry) offers rare insight. 'I asked where they thought I came from,' says Parry,

> but they displayed a similar lack of interest. Their translated reply came, 'We don't care where you come from because it's obviously crap! You can't climb trees, you've got no balance. We don't know what it is you wear on your body and feet, but it always seems to get in the way, it stays wet for ages and slows you up when you're hunting.'

Increasingly such distance is vanishing. Far-off villages are catching up with us and buying the shiny modern dream we sell so well, while many who've already bought it are smarting at not being able to get a refund.

The myth of travel is an interesting reminder of circularity. Two of the most popular stories about getting away from it all, *The Wizard of Oz* and *The Alchemist*, remind us that in searching high and low for treasure we find it right back where we started. The spiral offers learning, wisdom and transformation. We return home from our wanderings, the same but different. The god-like wizard is revealed to be a humble man, and the desired treasures of heart, brain and courage are located within us all the time. Jill Purce talks about the spiral movement of ages from the innocence of childhood where everything is connected, to the period of adolescence where ego separates us from everything else for personal gain. The next stage is the simple coming together again, where we realize how much we have in common and how much we can do in common. Perhaps this is the frontier of travel: the journey we are being asked to make out of one age and into another, journeying from division to a harmony within ourselves and between ourselves and the rest of creation.

Perhaps mapping the world with concrete, pylons, vapor trails and fly-overs was required, to help us realize that everything we need is with us already. Maybe we needed to jeopardize the health of our home to appreciate that the natural world here under our feet is as rich, beautiful and awe-inspiring as anything we could romanticize elsewhere. Perhaps we can now try to enjoy it without needing to fixate on owning it. Maybe all of us can share the world and, in so doing, not feel such suffocating alienation that we have to run off elsewhere in search of what's been lost.

The other part of our ability to travel comes when we are at our most stationary, or moving within the vehicle of our bodies. Meditation and dancing, shamanic journeying and dreaming, all provide us with daily opportunities to visit strange and alien lands, to explore spiritual dimensions that require neither passport nor inoculation. Living through his-story, we've pursued the most physical components of travel, but contained within each of us are unique and magical landscapes, the mapping and exploration of which offer inestimable value to us. There may be initial disappointment at the realization that our packaged tours are not giving us the feelings of freedom and transformation we were sold in the brochures. But how blessed to know we have the answers inside us; that we need neither money nor combustion engines nor pollution. Like the human passengers aboard the Axiom in the film *WALL·E,* all we need is to help each other remember how to walk.

Where's the Fire?

Fire has been brought in line like the rest of Nature; the genial pilot light, igniting gas and warming us with central heating systems; easy-strike matches and disposable lighters making the summoning and extinguishing of fire immediate and unthinking, like millions of obedient genii, demanded and forgotten at a moment's notice.

Since the 1960s, new buildings were erected in Britain lacking a place for fire. Some might be carved out, home to dried flowers or decorative stones, but most new homes find their heat at the flick of an electric switch. Even when fire is permitted, it's presented as a decoration, pretty but inessential next to the electric hub of the kitchen and the supplanting screens of computer and TV. The idea of actually cooking on a fire, let alone gathering round one in circle, seems archaic; the preserve of boy scouts and the occasional camping trip. In reality we are no less dependent on fire than we ever were, but like the best kind of servant, we've almost forgotten it's there.

The loss of our daily relationship with fire is one that parallels how much personal, familial and communal power we've handed over to a small handful of others. Fire is still key to the coal and nuclear power stations, but it's far away from our own fingers. The shared story round the fire has changed into the complex visions of films and TV programs, again controlled by the few and received passively by millions in their isolated rooms. The former focal point of the fire has moved from the center of the circle, sidelined by his-story to the edge of the room before being banished in favor of the blue flame of the TV and gloss-coated radiators. Cleaner, less threatening and far less communal, TV spreads its magic readymade. No flights of fancy spring out from its cold blue flicker. The fire of cooking that once brought everyone together to break bread and share food has likewise been removed. The kitchen, formerly considered a dull annex to the men's realm of *real* power, is now a box of electric-powered radiation, delivering food to us from elsewhere, pre-packaged, heavily preserved and available in portions for one. Heat is now dispensed through the walls in metal tubes raising one's temperature but not warming our hearts or our spirits. We have light bulbs and plug sockets, but given the ever rising number of people suffering from depression, we could be said to have lost our spark.

The loss of fire is the loss of our own power. As our potency has dimmed, so that of machines has grown, advertised as saving us the bother. The film *The Matrix* took root among many imaginations because of its implication that the machines we created as servants have become our masters. Unable to unplug ourselves from the vast machine, we stay where we are, impotent and complicit in its growth. The babies we celebrate bringing into the world are harnessed to it like fresh batteries. And the pictures we are sold, the message that happiness is a new car or wider television, convince us this situation works for us. When the thrill of consumption ebbs, we are presented with new decorations and components to upgrade our waning pleasure. Screens inside car headrests distract us from the growing tracts of dereliction and wilderness that pile up around the city limits. The fields under industrial monoculture, whose soil is so chemically treated and overworked, make Nature seem as chained to the churning engine and belching chimney as the rest of us. And the real impotence of trading our personal fire for the fire of technology and the national grid, becomes apparent only as we begin to question the dominant logic. As the RoboSapiens says in Jeanette Winterson's *The Stone Gods*, 'Humans have given away all their power to a "they". You aren't able to fight the system because without the system none of you can survive.'

This being his-story, the idea of man and machines is now presented as warfare, man *versus* machine in a techno battleground of one possible future. But machines aren't a great swarming enemy. Incapable of procreation without us empowering them, they are the versions of children the masculine has given birth to. Within such a heritage, man has once more omitted the soul from these machines. Scientifically unwilling to allow an animating spirit to either us or the natural world, whose minerals are used without respect, man's machines are only valued when new and working, dismissed and dismantled when old and erratic. They are traded in for younger models, in the way some men treat their spouses and families. And while fridges pile up in rusting heaps like modern dolmens, they stand as testimony to the greater sadness, which is how little man thinks of himself and what he has made of his day in the sun.

There is a deep sense of self-loathing about this attitude to machinery and hence to ourselves. Unaided by the feminine he has exorcized, the unsatisfied masculine wants to make the world perfect. When he sees the mess he is making, he gives the machine a kick and vows to try harder.

The humble reflection of machines is that ultimately we can switch them off. We have enormous power, more power than we are using, and only in the exercise of that power will return the remembrance of what it is to live. Like a patient in a hospital, we are eating, breathing and moving only with the assistance of a series of hums, the continual bleep of the machine, the invisible subtle energy of electricity. But we have to ask ourselves: is this living?

Fire is a living thing. Like us and even like the machines we have created to function for us, it consumes fuel and gives off waste. But whereas fire is natural, the impacting waste from our miraculous masculine machines is only beginning to be felt, and even then by those distant communities in places like China and Africa which process our waste. Across the world our redundant machines are shipped, with less ceremony and regret than befits their tireless service. They vanish in the trash or are deposited at council tips. If anything, we feel a shiver of relief. Across the seas they are dissected for serviceable parts and metals by cultures aspiring to be like us. Many of them are burnt, as the simplest means of breaking them down and getting at their vital components. And the smell is ...

Most of us have smelt burning plastic (the end of a pen in an idle moment at the school Bunsen burner, for instance): it's about as far from the enticing smell of wood smoke as it's possible to get. Unlike tobacco leaves, our plastic products don't come with a health warning. But in those areas of the world taking and burning our plastic waste, the toxic plumes remind some of the hidden costs contained in our mass-produced plasticity. Buried or burnt, the graves of our discarded toys are mounting up. And the further we go down the disposable path, the bigger the cost to our ecosystem and our species' future.

Cars are another example of our reliance on the spark of life, taken from our hands and given to something else. Hidden in engines, the little fires we drive around in are fuelled by the Earth and pollute the air, while at the same time furthering the erosion of our own sense of personal power. The simple practice of putting one foot in front of the other now appears exhausting. And while our personal health suffers from lack of exercise, increased stress and intolerance towards others, so the plight of our world worsens. It seems a false dream to make our electricity-dependent culture reliant on huge renewable energy systems, when so many of our personal and communal losses would remain. Wind, solar and water power are only compatible if accompanied by a rethink in how we craft and look after the machines these forces are intended to power. If we aren't encouraged to see all aspects of the world as living, we will still discard and dispose when they fail our rigid definitions of working. Rather than fixate on what power sources can best keep our mechanical wheels turning, we would do well to remember how it was that our ancestors managed to survive and thrive so successfully, without either raping the Earth for materials or poisoning her with pollutants.

The skill of lighting a fire has become marginalized and yet no other single skill offers us any chance of a future. Our personal power is as precious as the strike of flint on tinder, as delicate and inherent to our survival anywhere on Earth. With that successful spark comes the capacity for food, warmth, illumination and companionship (fires attract people to open up, joke and sing, as strongly as TV alienates and silences us). The humble brew, so daily taken for granted at the flick of a switch, would be nothing were it not for our capability as fire-makers. Together with finding fresh water and knowing what leaves and berries to eat, being able to make fire secures our future more than philosophy, science or law.

To understand how every aspect of our life involving a lack of energy expended on our part has lost a vital component of its becoming, may help to show how much power we have given up. It is no wonder we may feel (though comfortable, waited on and entertained at the press of a switch) as useless as lords of misrule: as though the fire has gone out of us. Reclaiming this power will involve more effort, but it also promises us back a sense of purpose. We will begin to remember exactly how much we are capable of. Renewing our connections with the physical and spiritual worlds, we will be able to access gratitude and wonder, instead of being skilled in impatience and boredom. There's so much we've got used to, and how many of us are brave enough to unplug from the mains and plug ourselves back into the Earth before we have to? One thing is certain: it's not going to be possible unless we come together more than we currently do. We are creatures of society because only with each other can we become more than the sum of our individual parts.

We have choice. At the moment we have so much choice it could almost be said we're spoiled for it. And while the system runs and the money flows and the plugs work, which of us needs to think otherwise?

Maybe we could start by more actively engaging with our machines, like all our tools, like our friends and the elements; valuing their help, listening to their gripes, heeding them when they tell us to switch off and go and do something more interesting instead.

And making sure we remember how to start a fire.

Owning it All

In 1969 man walked on the moon. Even if you number yourself among those who believe man got as far as walking across a TV studio, the effect of the footage was enormous. Our home shrank and the universe expanded. *Star Trek* earlier proclaimed the pioneering spirit, with the final frontier crossed by those who would boldly go where no 'man' had gone before. But what purpose did it serve for man to stand on the moon? Was it to show mankind's supremacy over other creatures in creating the means to leave his home world behind? Was it to venture forth to new planets; carrying the tools and ideas of his-story and, as colonialism had done with the home world, bringing them on message if they appeared to do things differently? Maybe it was to signify the ultimate triumph over the feminine; as if to say 'Look at your symbol, the moon; we're walking all over her!'

Not long after the moon landing I came into the world. One of my most treasured books as a child was written by Michael Foreman and called *Dinosaurs and All That Rubbish*. The book spoke of a man who lived in paradise but whose attention was fixed elsewhere, on a star that shone in the sky. His obsession with reaching the star caused forests to be cut down, replaced with factories and towering mounds of rubbish. Reaching the moon mightn't have been the engine behind the development of agriculture, the building of castles and the industrial revolution, but it seems to me to be the same drive: born of masculine single-mindedness and a sense of division, hand in hand with the concept of private ownership. Minerals were free to be taken by man, and Nature was dismissed as separate and dumb enough to be exploited.

One of the most significant emblems of this idea of ownership was a square piece of fabric on a pole. The flag, whatever colors and shapes starred on it, was used to mark territory. Planting it in jungle, field or on the moon said the same thing: 'This belongs to us.' One of the most common responses of indigenous people to the arrival of white settlers with their developed system of ownership (and flags) was bafflement. How was it possible to own part of the land, as Chief Seattle asked in 1854, when 'every part of this soil is sacred', when our bodies themselves are on loan, and when the care of the Earth is a responsibility for future generations that requires tenderness and humility, not legally binding documents?

Ownership of the material world is what his-story has excelled at. In economics there's a graph for the exchange between opportunity and costs. An economy can put its energy into milk or butter, or find a place somewhere in the middle, where the individual bulk of either choice is reduced so both can be enjoyed. The result of choosing an *either/or* path, rather than balancing both, has brought us to this point of extremes. On the one hand, our cult of ownership has brought unparalleled material wealth. We have roads, vehicles to drive on them, fuel to power them. We have clothes, furnishings and objects; enough to allow multi cults of fashion to develop. We have constructed huge metropolises, diverted and damned rivers, and generated electricity. We have created a system of entertainment so successful we have more books, films, songs and games than there are hours to consume them. We have a system of money that makes more money simply by virtue of itself. We have a globe of cuisine available in a matter of seconds. We have holidays, swimming pools and hot tubs. We have goose feather duvets and intelligent foam pillows. We have tablets to subdue pain, relieve stress and help us sleep. We have legislation, traffic lights, wet suits, skinny de-caf cappuccinos and Sky Plus.

The list of material gains in the march of progress is beyond reckoning, and though I could easily go on, the intention of this is not to replicate the Argos catalogue. In short, materially, we do indeed have it all. According to opportunity cost analysis, we are off the scale.

And yet ...

Isaac Newton said, 'For every action there is an equal and opposite reaction.' The culmination of every stage of development along the unfolding narrative of his-story is available for all of us to witness. This is the place where the march of material progress has brought us. Every pollutant, every awkwardly resilient piece of plastic debris, every piece of property with its attendant concepts of envy and greed, every war, has no other cause than the persistent tendency to unbalance, divide and conquer over the last 5,000 years. We choose the paths we take; we must accept responsibility for where they lead us.

'Progress' is an interesting word, nestling closely yet far away from its sister word, 'process'. For much of the ideology that has fueled this masculine culture, the idea of progress has been a glittering trophy, giving weight to spade, and persistence to invention. Progress is linear. Lives will be longer, food will be cheaper, surround-sound systems will be louder. Process is cyclical, like the water cycle. Rains fall, rivers run, seas warm, clouds gather, rains fall. Nowhere in this cycle do we get a sense of preference or bias. Nowhere does Nature attempt to speed things up, refine the quality or harry the languid meander of a river. Nowhere in Nature's way is there any waste. Yet over this period, we have favored intervention and innovation, believing each step further off the path of harmony to be one step nearer a concept of perfection we can see but somehow Nature can't.

There's a piece of art in the Tate Modern in London by Kathy Prendergast called 'Lost'. It is a map of North America naming only those place with the word 'lost' in the title: Lost Brook, Lost Spring, Lost Creek. What has been lost during this long, alienating and sickening march of progress is the health of the natural world we must live with to survive. It is a sentiment elucidated by the famous Cree Indian proverb: 'Only when the last tree has died and the last river been polluted and the last fish caught will we realize we cannot eat money.'

Progress doesn't do loss. But it is becoming increasingly clear that for everything we have gained, something equally vital has been lost. What we have lost is the spiritual, which cannot be bought or sold. Individually and collectively we have pursued a path of imbalance that furnishes us with luxuries while threatening our elemental needs. Water is more polluted, the air less breathable, the Earth more poisoned. The growth of the human species has come at the expense of every other. Our sense of separation grows, as does our fear at what will become of us. We feel, at our most primal and irrational, a sense of unquiet at everything we have. We intuit that all is far from bountiful, that the pact we made has some unread clauses. Car adverts begin to chill; their vision of the deserted road empty but for a solitary car strikes a disingenuous note with the snarling, raging jams of reality. The smiling wrap of perfumed laundry itches against our increasingly allergic skin. The digital television channels proliferate, but show only repeats. We are beginning to tug at the stray thread of the Emperor's New Clothes and don't know which is more galling: that the fabric unravels so easily, or that we might have to step onwards without its illusion to clothe us?

The paradox with ownership is that once we think we have something, we no longer value it. In Foreman's book, the man believes he *owns* the planet. He then has to find something else to occupy him and looks to the distant star. This fascination with something other than what we already have is the core discontent ruining the gift of this planet. We have imprisoned ourselves in cages of ownership, with our sofa beds and dining tables (not for nothing are they called *trappings*). And awareness of this in one part of the world comes at a time when the ideology of ownership and exploitation is taking off in those parts of the world that until recently only knew the exploitation. People might be working for pennies a day to make clothes for high-street stores, but they understand the importance of saving those pennies to own a Gucci handbag. They have caught our illness of dissatisfaction; they have developed the disease of aspiration. They have spotted the star in the sky and want to reach it. We might have shackled ourselves to disease and disaffection, but the advertising of the shackles is so successful, even the remotest parts of the globe are now buying it.

To reach the star, the man decimates the environment to build a rocket. Like the Earth in Foreman's story, our environment has been trashed by a party of ungrateful humanity on a global scale. Pollution and waste are so prevalent that all I can guarantee is that between me putting these words down and you reading them, the damage will have multiplied. And the painful reality is that we haven't yet accepted the situation fully to move on to the next step: how to stop it. Like Mickey Mouse in *The Sorcerer's Apprentice,* our tricks to bring the system under control only seem to be making it worse. Writer Alison Benjamin is not alone when she says, 'Imagining that science will somehow come to our rescue shows a spectacular failure to comprehend the scale of the crisis.' To look further in the direction of unbalanced science is untenable. We have reached the limit of error. There is no new tablet to cure this.

In James Lovelock's book *Gaia* he speaks of the Earth as an interconnected and living being, in which all that we do feeds back on itself. 'In our belief that all that matters is the good of humankind we foolishly forget how much we depend upon all the other living things of Earth.' If you upset the natural harmony, then upset and disharmony follow. In a closed circuit, there is no 'somewhere else' to dump the unwanted by-products of our endeavors.

We will never find our peace if we continue to subscribe to the idea that our natural birthright is fundamentally flawed and in need of improvement. This is our home and she is perfect. We have lived for 5,000 years with an idea that spoke the contrary and as a result we have made her sick. Our priority must be to make her well again. Foreman's remedy in the book is for the dinosaurs to come back and tidy up the land to make it habitable for life. Perhaps the dinosaurs are waiting to re-emerge, to trample all the fossil-derived plastics back into black mulch. Perhaps the dinosaurs symbolize Nature. Given half the chance, Nature creeps back, through roads, up buildings, pulling down the grandest designs of humanity as the sea defeats sandcastles. With a creative vision and low-impact involvement from all of us, Nature will be eager to help us with the process of tidying up: repairing the grossly broken fabric of the world; singing back the bees, sea currents and coral; restoring to all life a world where everything works. My cousin bought a smallholding 20 years ago. There was an oak tree growing where the previous owner regularly tipped the chemicals he used to dip his sheep. The oak tree looked as miserable as it's possible for a tree to look and still have its roots in the ground. Twenty years without sheep dip and the oak tree is beaming. As the fear of owning up to what we are doing paralyzes us, we need to remember that it is never too late.

The poetry of Foreman's story comes when the man reaches his long-cherished star, to find he's exchanged verdant life for a big lump of rock, uninhabitable and unimpressive. Oh, he thinks, what a disappointment. It would be glorious to see all the advancements of mankind as ushering in a wonderful new world. If I switched on the news to see great tales of happiness, peace and fulfillment then I wouldn't have been told to write this book. But the more man shapes and affects the world, the more defaced she becomes. To let Nature help us recover we have to desist from so persistently crippling her.

Even with a wealth of elementals, spirit helpers and gods to remember, their roles are dependent on us listening to their wisdom and using our own physical form to put it into practice. We have to make the next steps ourselves. We have to come back from outer space, like the man in Foreman's story, and begin again to tend the home we've been gifted, with mouths to feed and babies gurgling and the elderly to mind. When the man does leave his space rock to travel to yet another distant star, he finds a beautiful world, alive with plants and animals. A dinosaur tells him this planet is Earth. Shock hits the man, who can't believe the transformation, and he asks for a small piece of it to call his own. The dinosaur informs him that he can't have a bit of it, he can have all of it, as long as he shares it with all other life. 'Don't be ridiculous,' says the man. 'You can't tell me what to do; you've got a brain the size of a pea.'

Nature responds with the dinosaur: 'My brain might be small, but my heart is bigger than yours.'

There are those who find it easier to believe in the establishment of colonies on the moon than the return of the dinosaurs. And yet on page 1715 of a recent Argos catalogue, under the sub-section 'Robotics', is a creature called Pleo:

> Pleo is a one-week old infant Camarasaurus from the Jurassic period and is an authentic Life Form! He will let you know how he feels, as he is capable of actual emotions including joy, aggression, sorrow, and fear. He can also yawn, sigh, sniff, sniffle, snore, cough, hiccup and sneeze. Includes rechargeable batteries.

It is £230 worth of wonder to witness a craze for a creature capable of expressing emotion, given how much emotion-expressing life can exist on Earth. If we want the joy of creatures with all the wild, glorious, lovable aspects of life we claim for ourselves, we need to stop deluding ourselves that we can make them better with batteries.

His-story has charted 5,000 years of separation and ownership, making it difficult to see this world as something for all life to share and enjoy. We're so used to the right to buy, whether houses or cars, that we get edgy if a fly finds its way in through a window. How far removed we've strayed from the idea of living in harmony with other creatures, whatever they look like, whatever noises they make! And yet, if we are to begin to help our home recover we will benefit from letting Nature in all her forms reclaim her position. We might need to accept that rather than do more to the planet, we need to do less. We may need to listen to the other stories that Nature is trying to tell us.

To move on, to find our way back to the Garden, to release our shackles of trappings and to heal the many wounds, both personal and ecological, requires not denial but one great act of ownership. We need to own up that every problem we are currently witnessing is due to our own ideas and plots. It is an ownership in the true sense. Not a 'BOGOF' bargain. Not another piece of tinsel or a bigger car. This is spiritual ownership of our mistakes. We need to own the warfare, suffering and poverty, not to struggle to perfect more clever machines to carry the can and tidy up for us. We need to view everything around us, including our fellow creatures, as examples of life as precious as ourselves, to respect and value. This ownership requires us to accept that carving up the Earth has caused the fractures and schisms that beset us. We need to own that money is not essential for living, that life was once possible without it and will be again. To own, as the male Aboriginals in Australia have done recently, that a massive apology is due to the grandmothers of this planet.

Like flags, guns, leasehold tenancy agreements, remote controls and mobile phones, this ownership is in our hands. We need to own up to our own role in furthering the divisions and inequalities, to own up for the actions of our forefathers who laid this track over the thousands of years before us and signed away our rights to dwell everywhere on this shared planet. We might not have started the fire, but what we do with it is now in no one else's hands but ours. We can put them up. We can accept responsibility for it all, together, every one of us. We can do it. We have the power.

It is this power of choice that belongs to every one of us.

For the Wheel to Turn

It is in the nature of wheels to turn. Embracing our place as one of the many creatures in the natural world returns us to a sense of circularity. In the spiral of the seasons and the cycle of water, all life is in the round. Like the circle of arrows in the recycling symbol, we are being led back to the place from which we came. What this spiraling circularity can give us is the reassurance that for all the mess of this last age, things must change.

The wheel of our year is naturally spoked with festivals that mark the movement of the sun. Seasonal celebrations within many cultures cluster around these same natural turning points: two solstices, two equinoxes, and the quarter days between them. By honoring these sabbats (holy days) we ground ourselves in our home and the presence of the circle.

The importance of the Yule festival around the Winter Solstice (December 21st) is to provide a time of feasting, drinking and community at the darkest point of the year. The slender snowdrop of hope at Imbolc (February 1st) is the promise of renewal. It is around this date that Tibetan, Chinese and Iroquois cultures celebrate their new year. The Vernal Equinox (March 21st) marks the first of the two balancing days in the year where days and nights are equal. This is the beginning of spring and is named Ostara after the goddess of fecundity and new life (from which we get Easter and the symbolism of eggs). Beltane (May 1st) is a fertility festival that encourages sex and impregnation across the land to germinate the seeds.

The Summer Solstice (June 21st) is the height of summer, and Glastonbury festival provides an example of what can be expected at this time of year: long parties, large gatherings and not much sleep. Lammas (August 1st) is so-called to celebrate the first loaf of the year, beginning the season of reaping and picking which culminates with Harvest at the Autumn Equinox

(September 21st), a time of gratitude for the abundance of the year, before the year winds down to its close at Samhain (October 31st). Samhain affords people the chance to ritualize what they want to let go of from the outgoing year and remember the ancestors who have passed over before them. It's a time of respect for the dead, for their gifts of life, wisdom and compassion. In addition to the solar sabbats there are the lunar festivals, celebrating the monthly passage of the moon. These sacred days can be variously given over to bathing, fasting, feasting and journeying. All these festivals are necessary if we want to find our way back into a harmonious relationship with life.

The need for festivities is as primal as our need to dance, to make-believe, to feel empowered and to gather. Festivals connect us more intimately with each other and the world and give life meaning. They ground us in the movements of sun, moon, planets and stars and reveal how they impact on our existence. They bond us to the wisdom of our ancestors and remind us of the joy that is written into the heart of life.

Everywhere we look, the world shows itself in the round. Life blossoms towards death and returns anew. Day segues into night and back to day. The frailty of a young baby grows strong and capable in adulthood before collapsing into frailty again. Tides ebb and flow, the moon waxes and wanes, our breaths rise and fall, and blood is pumped lemniscatically round our body. In all of these motions there is up and down, in and out, quiet and loud, and as many other dancing partners as we choose to make. There is flux, there is movement, and we find our rhythm with it. Circular time is asking to be restored to its place of meaning after thousands of years of belittlement.

To embrace circularity is to be invited to join the whole world, to see ourselves as holistic beings of mind, body and spirit, different from and equal with every other aspect of life. We have a rich capacity to experience, share and understand, without setting ourselves apart in judgment of it. Allowing for the world to be circular, spectacular and varied helps us to see that *different* does not mean *evil*.

While some may complain about the loss of absolute standards of spelling and grammar, the freewheeling of a round world brings us back to poetry, myth and song. These go further in giving us a deeper and more ancient version of the world. Metaphor provides a path to the primitive feelings of the unconscious parts of our minds. Ambiguity, the meaning of two apparently different interpretations of the same thing, is the wealth of poetry. What is and what is not, being the same and different, dancing together across our skies, allows the world to deepen in resonance and possibility; allows for transformation and miracles. We will benefit from seeing fertility in the fecal, seeing the adult in the child and the child in the adult; engaging with the spiritual, energetic and subtle as much as the physical and material; marveling at how the ordinary, at every moment, is so much more.

Even as this is written, the wheel turns. The infinite possibilities of spiritual existence are returning, and one of the most powerful tools representing this renewal is the Internet. Living 'among the web', the virtual world invites us to connect with the ethereal and spiritual. It affords us the chance to experiment with other personas, as the idea of a single character dissolves in an unfolding cyberspace of imagination and avatars. Unlike the physical excess that has led to land ownership, property and cupboards full of stuff, we cannot hold onto the virtual, much as we can't hold onto the spiritual. Like a butterfly, the spiritual moves around and through us. To try and gas, catch and frame it is to kill it.

The virtual web is like the web of a spider: powerful, intricate and ephemeral, more easily brushed off than kept as proof. So if the World Wide Web offers us a gift, it is in the way it encourages us to reconnect with the immaterial. We can be transformed by experiences that are everywhere and nowhere. We can move through situations less in a straight line and more randomly. Chance signs on the street, unplanned meetings, snatched pieces of conversation, are like surfing from the link of one page to another. Many of the links we discover can never be retraced. The energy that powers computers is as eccentric as the energy of the world. We can enter. We can leave. We can experience. But we can't manufacture it to behave according to some pre-planned intention; we can't dictate whether it opens or not. We are players but we do not have dominion over the field. We only have responsibility for our own actions and for the choices we make.

The more we explore and engage, the more we learn about ourselves. Because the less there is certainty about others, the more we have to accept that, like the dark mirror of an inactive screen, what we are being shown is our own reflection. All aspects of our lives offer us reflection. How we behave in the world tells us who we are; the World Wide Web even more so, because (just like the spiritual practices of meditation and shamanic journeying) it offers imagined landscapes that are shaped uniquely by our personal experiences with it. And the empowerment of this tool comes from the realization that when we accept who we are through what we are shown, we can decide what to embrace and what to transmute.

Virtual communities are no substitute for physical communities, but since Mrs. Thatcher declared there was no such thing as society in the 1980s, some community is preferable to none at all. The popularity of social networking sites like Facebook and Twitter reveals how important it is for us to belong. We gain much from contributing to support networks for each other, whatever our ideas, tastes in music or sense of humor. These communities do not feel like the last attempt of this age to separate, so much as the seeds of the next. The transition from virtual to physical communities is still young, but it feels like a rebirth of those timeless tribal societies that remind us how we can live together with the Earth.

Attempts over the last 40 years to set up intentional communities across this island along environmental and spiritual lines have been brave beginnings. There is nothing so challenging as to chop wood and carry water when the system is still functioning enough for you to pop to Sainsbury's for a bap. Many of the communities number around a dozen, and the oft-mentioned number for a workable tribe is around 144 (or 12 families of 12). This can seem bizarre to people used to seeing hundreds of faces on their daily commute, only to return to living alone. But to mend the world needs us to return to the circle, to offer help and support, to ease the burdens and share the wealth, to remember how much we are given by loving and feeling loved by those around us.

The importance of tribal groupings is to make community more practical. Part of the aim of the Transition Movement is to sow these seeds of community among people at the level of the small town and large village; helping them to bring power back into their hands; giving them their say in how their particular world will look and function, as they decide what is *true* for them.

The linguistic victory of his-story was how it co-opted truth as its alibi, against which any dissent was *false*. But deciding what is true (the foundation on which all stories rest) lies with the power of our personal belief. This ability to make-believe, if it is to empower us, rather than merely control and direct us, sits in our ability to develop a body of memory of personal experience free from intimidation. In our exploration of the world, our minds and bodies are capable of having direct, unfiltered personal experiences. These experiences count. They are our personal and communal truths in the world. No other person can tell us what to feel. No one can take the power of our own beliefs away from us, however different they may be. As information levels reach overload, our brains perform a miraculous function. We shut out the irrelevant and allow through only the important. The range and variety of characters and interests mean there is no unified theory of belief, which everyone and everything can be shoehorned into. One person's Madonna is another's Nirvana.

Sitting around the fire with our children, our ancestors, our animals and our spirits, we need to hear stories. These stories can bring us together, whether we're being told them on a world that grew from the back of a giant turtle or one that was summoned into being by a snake charmer. They give us communion and we each have them, like collections of stumbled-upon stones from all the shores we've crossed. They are the stories that need to be heard and shared now. As we take back our power, we discover our voices. The uniform has become ripped. All the other stories that his-story has negated and derided are returning. These are the stories of the feminine, the stories of other cultures, of other creatures, the stories of other sexualities and other bodies; of other practices and other ideas. Not his-story, but our stories.

Winging its way on the curve of a ball across a pitch, the spiritual, like the circle, is returning. As we feel the validity of the immaterial as much as the physical, as we celebrate the organic and natural in harmony with our tools and craft, so we turn to face one of the greatest fears that has for so long turned us against our life: Death.

In the wheel of the year, death is as central a force as life. Our fear around Hallowe'en is the wasteful energy of running from that which is natural and comes to all of us. But it's understandable. The notion of hell succeeded in mobilizing us to extreme work-patterns. When science got rid of the soul, death became the absolute end. Life became frightening to a system that had no story of reincarnation or spiritual succor. If this is all we get, so the logic goes, we better hold on tight. In Todd Haynes' film *Safe*, Julianne Moore plays a woman so frightened of dying she creates a hermetic shield in her home: not so much living as avoiding death. But our obsession with unnaturally sterile environments has been cited as one of the main reasons for the rise in allergies and the weakening of our immune systems. Denied the chance to learn immunity, we have perversely become more vulnerable to illness.

Death is the unwritten clause that accompanies our incarnation on Earth. Our choice is whether we build a world based on fearing it, or one that celebrates and honors it. The return of the spiritual asks us to revive our imaginations; to recall stories of the individual life essence in every living thing, returning to and arriving from a place called, perhaps, 'the land of the dead', to re-incarnate again. Dare we live each day to the full, knowing that one day our physical being will rot? Can we remember ways to honor the signs of aging as markers signifying depth, wisdom and understanding? Can we believe that though our bodies have to die, something will one day return?

How we perceive death reflects how we view life. The mass availability of cosmetic surgery, aimed at keeping us looking unlined by age, suggests we are not keen to look in the mirror and see death approaching. Instead we shut our eyes to death, increasingly immune to news tallies of war victims, the distant starving and the millions killed by dis-ease; scared to death of reaching that doorway. Our fear of dying is not merely a tangent to pressing concerns; it is an active complicity in how we shape our future. The less brave we feel, the more cowed into cowardice we become, the more content we are to let a few individuals in power dictate the path we must follow. The courage of thousands of people in Egypt in 2011 was explained in terms of them overcoming their fear of death. Having done that, there was nothing left to fear. As a result they changed their world.

This period of transition is asking all of us to take back our power: to rekindle the fire within us and to make those changes that can help more than just us. Engaging fully with the world shows us the magnificent giantess of Nature that can crush us, but also her delicate magic that inexplicably rescues us: the branches that catch us, the water that cushions us, the miracles waiting at every turn to defy convention and affirm the existence of the impossible. It is in the wild that life and death dance close. Accidents do happen, and daring to die means daring to live. By refusing to look at death, we feed fear and imagine everything is out to destroy us. Like the *Final Destination* films, we imbue Death with a perverse form of revenge, glorifying her as an arch-tyrant, instead of seeing her like the shopkeeper in *Mr. Benn,* genially appearing when it's time for us to return to that place from which we came.

Those who face their fears return emboldened, invigorated and confident; they have expressions that convey they've come face to face with Death, met her stare without blinking, put their head in her noose, dived into the tidal wave. Such bravery turns us from worriers to warriors. To feel the fear is to gain an understanding of fear's limits and the spiritual messages long cherished by our ancestors, that death is just a crossing. When we see the cycle of life and death in the round, we know that for all the decay, life will return. Like the February fires that mark the awakening new year, after death must come life.

Ending at the Beginning

Hello again! How was that? Hopefully it's left you more inspired than depressed, if for no other reason than showing that at last the boys are catching up! But it's understandable if reading through a catalogue of his-story, covering 5,000 years at a fair old lick, might leave you wondering whether to take a large quantity of pills or throw yourself under the next passing train. It can be tricky, this transitioning process. Sometimes it can all feel a bit too much and part of you stresses and asks 'Is this the end of the world?' To which my answer would be 'Yes, but don't panic because it's also the beginning of another.'

What exactly is coming next can prompt as many answers as there are mouths suggesting it. Will the dinosaurs return? Will insects take over the planet? Will humanity mutate into unexpected forms to cope with chemical pollution? Will people in any form survive?

For some, the future has already been prophesied in the bibles of his-story. Many Christians in America are readying themselves for Rapture; the moment when they are teleported to Heaven while the Earth undergoes just what it needs: the upheaval of more battles between *good* and *evil*. For others, growing ecological problems prophesy a range of global crises that suggest all life on Earth faces turbulent times. Some see the world continuing much like it is, with technology stepping in to create safe zones in which hermetic living becomes ever more necessary, while the outside world sinks into a wasteland. Others see the changes as emblematic of a shift in vibration, raising the consciousness of the world to higher dimensions of nice-sounding stuff like world peace and divine love. Whatever your interpretation of the numbers 2012, the sense that something momentous is unfolding seems tangible.

But what is to come feels shrouded: not just prevented from

being seen, but as yet unwritten, dependent on all our actions over the coming years. The future, our own and that of our planet, is in our hands. And the more aware of this we become, the more exposed seem the corners in which we hoped to hide away. The sand is blown clear and we can no longer bury our heads in it. We are being asked to look up and accept the elephant in the room that was created from our endeavors and those of our ancestors. We have the choice. We can choose to ignore it and be complicit in the continuation of suffering and destruction. We can choose to accept it and change. But at the end of the world, it's up to us.

The importance of choice is something that has reappeared through capitalism. Opening life up to the variety of the market has encouraged us to exercise choice. We no longer receive what we are given from on high, but decide whether we want beans or peas for tea. Yet capitalism also shows its limitations, rewarding the brutal and unethical to keep the hierarchies of this age in place; demanding payment for what is available free of charge. As we begin to experience ethical consumption, we feel our choices change. We understand that convenient plastic bags will migrate to throttle sea turtles. We are invited to make another choice: between destroying our selves and our home, and repairing it. If this moment of life on Earth can be summed up, it is between the end of one world and the mend of another.

Choosing local broccoli might seem minute next to the survival of the ocean currents, but small acts are as intrinsic to the health of the whole as a single vein is to the entire bloodstream. We have to start somewhere, and recognizing our power and potential (in however small a way) is the first step to bigger changes. Now we are choosing to carry a recycled cloth bag to the supermarket. Over the coming few years we will be asked to choose the continued existence of supermarkets themselves.

I'm putting these lines down on Earth Day, in the spring of 2011, when the very existence of a day to celebrate the Earth feels radically hopeful. Revolutions have been spinning in North Africa and the Middle East, and across the globe a single word is uniting students in London with protestors in Yemen with strikers in Mexico: Solidarity! Examples of continued injustice are prompting demonstrations at everything from despotism and the blatant injustice of capital greed, to how we fish. It seems that, in the words of Burmese pro-democracy campaigner Aung San Suu Kyi, 'people are becoming aware of their own potential.'

Economically, any attempt by the current global financial system to plug the hole in its hull only reminds us of how unseaworthy it is. And the spread of digital technology is not just helping people to organize, it is providing a continual reminder to those clinging on to oversized portions of power that their every blink is now under popular surveillance.

Ecologically our attitudes are changing. The Co-Operative is planting 'Bee roads' of wild flowers across the UK, to restore some of the 97% of wildflower meadows lost since the 1930s. And growing numbers of saplings reveal that more fields are being turned back to broadleaf woodland. On a cultural level, there are frequent examples of boys being helped to recognize the limitations of laddishness, through TV programs like *Tool Academy* and *How to Live with Women*. And there is the sublime manifesto at the beginning of Lady Gaga's *Born This Way* video: a reminder that if anyone has been put here to help men get over their fear of death it may well be Mother Monster herself!

Whatever is coming, we need to remember that we are, in the words of David Tennant's incarnation of *Doctor Who*, 'brilliant'. It has taken great human inventiveness and determination to bring about the world we inhabit. We can assure ourselves that we have just such qualities to shift us out of fear and defeatism into whatever is next. I believe it is with our roles as individuals that we start. We have the chance to shape our days on the most ordinary levels. We can decide to stay in judgment of others, blindly acting out examples of our own pain and suffering. We can also practice accepting these judgments as our own reflection (hard at first, but gets easier and eventually can even be funny), and heed their lessons and grow. We can choose whether we direct our inner monsters, raging and screaming and hurting, at one another. But we can also find ways, through dance, performance, drumming, ritual and healing, to express what we don't need safely, and, in the words of a friend of mine, 'give it to the universe'. We can choose how we work, how we live, how we love. And at each turn, through practice, through a renewed connection with our spiritual essence that links us with every other life form on the planet, we can encourage this; being patient, kind and compassionate to ourselves and each other. In the words of another friend, Liz, who read this book when it was still in draft form, 'I think we're all in nappies on this one – all super young in our confidence, imagination and belief in how we can shape our lives in a way that's more organic, in tune and connected.' This is how things begin: with nappies, baby steps, tremendous chutzpah and not a few stumbles.

But we are not just individuals. We are parts of families, members of communities, aspects of a wider world of other animals, plants and elements. Equally important is realizing there are thousands, millions of us, who are making these steps together; aware of change and the need for it, keen to support each other as we begin to mend. There are many examples of people coming together in communities all over the world. In India, Auroville is a thriving body of 50,000 members, working towards human unity in diversity, whose core principles of sustainability, transformation through consciousness, and social spiritual existence are helping people to reforest the land and live in harmony. In the UK, the movement towards Transition is spreading its ideas of how to help us away from oil dependency at this time of climatic shift. The guildelines of working at a holistic and group level, with creative education, resilience, relocalization, hope and engagement, are empowering increasing numbers of groups. Central to this idea of 'transitioning' is the belief that as individuals we have the solutions and together we can put them into practice. Whether our communities number tens of thousands or just ten, the more we reach out and find the hands of those next to us, the more positive and capable we feel. Together we can help and be helped, and to believe it, to afford it that jewel of human consciousness and even know it, is to harness the energy of possibility.

And these ideas do not stop at the level of village, tribe or small town. Our world of more than 6 billion people is showing itself ready and committed to change. Across the Earth, a band of thirteen indigenous grandmothers met in October 2004 to form an alliance. Thirteen women from traditional medicine peoples were brought together to remind us of what must be central to this transition. They believe that the ancestral ways of prayer, peace-making and healing are vitally needed today, and have come together to nurture, educate and train our children. They join with all those who honor the healing of Mother Earth, for all our relations. Even further back, at the request of the United Nations World Commission on Environment and Development in 1987, the writers of *The Earth Charter* put forward a paper whose core principles are simple and universal: the respect and care for the community of life; ecological integrity; social and economic justice; democracy, non-violence and peace. The renewal they ask for 'requires a change of mind and heart. It requires a new sense of global interdependence and universal responsibility. We must imaginatively develop and apply the vision of a sustainable way of life, locally, nationally, regionally and globally'.

But one of the most heartening seedlings I've come across recently is the news that Bolivia is about to pass the world's first laws granting all Nature equal rights to those of humans. Full of language that wouldn't look out of place among that of the Na'vi of Pandora, from the film *Avatar*, the Law of Mother Earth will establish 11 new rights including the right to life and to exist; the right to continue vital cycles and processes free from human alteration; the right to pure water and clean air; the right not to be polluted and the right to balance. It is a fine trumpet call to governments and communities, leaders and tribes across the world as to how to take those first baby steps towards remembering how our ancestors once lived.

We're all different and everyone is needed – from artists and scientists to teachers and healers. In the words of the Charter, 'Let ours be a time remembered for the awakening of a new reverence for life.'

For all the problems of this particular narrative of humanity, it is our humanity that will rescue us. For what are we, as people, if not a living embodiment of the marriage between heaven and earth, between the animal parts of us that roar and devour and the astral parts of us that love unconditionally. As people, we have the capacity to affect the world around us. We have shown how we can plow the Earth into ruin. Now let us sing her back into health.

The process of change requires us to gain some things and lose others. The opportunity facing all of us is to decide what stays and what goes. For those who bore witness to the collapse of the Twin Towers in 2001, modern technology provided insight into what, faced with impending death, people chose to carry with them as their parting words: truly their last testament. Those three words, 'I Love You', repeated, cried and whispered, prove all that is ever needed. Love. The heart of wisdom. Choosing to understand instead of judge, to forgive instead of accuse, and to embrace instead of reject. Our love is the most important item we can take with us. Next to losing love, wouldn't most of us agree to give up polythene? If we have love, we can find food, build fire, source water and sleep sound. Are we ready to put down all the holy texts, to remember there are plants and animals prepared to teach us, and a great big planet always willing to hold us?

If this book has any value, it is to remind us that the last age has been a cultural creation and, as such, it has a beginning and will have an end. As Chief Seattle said in the 19th century, 'This time of decay may be distant, but it will surely come, for even the White Man, whose God walked and talked with him as friend to friend, cannot be exempt from the common destiny.' In the 1980s, Gerda Lerner wrote that the time of patriarchy 'seems to have nearly run its course'. As the ground beneath us shakes, we are reminded that we are witnessing the momentous and imminent end to a 5,000-year process. This is the lowest, heaviest part of the cycle. We are meant to rise again. As the journey of the spiral demonstrates, we separate so that we may come together. This is what it means to 'remember' – literally to re-member: to bring ourselves back together.

To those of us terrified about this transition, there is little advice better than Sue Jeffer's adage to 'feel the fear and do it anyway'. For without acknowledging our fear of the unknown, we will never experience the wonder at our own power; our ability to rise to these challenges; to feel our way through the world anew and to embrace the buds of this immortal Tree of Life. By facing our fears, we most truly experience love. By daring to express remorse, passion, anger and sadness, we begin to understand what has taken place. By recognizing the crimes of this age and by showing compassion and forgiveness to the people and ideologies that perpetrated them, we successfully let them go. By letting go of what holds us back, we can really move on.

And to those of us who intuit what is unfolding, it is our choice and our responsibility to make that move now: to reclaim our lives and re-member ourselves as living parts of a bigger picture. Not his-story but the whole story.

The rounding of a circle brings us back to how the world lived before his-story took hold. It offers a return to harmony; to a balance between work and play, between the masculine and feminine, between men and women, between our individuality and the health and vitality of the community; between people and the rest of life; between the as above and the so below. What this age, at once both new and ancient, offers us is the chance to consciously shape it with every thought, word and action.

And in mending the Earth, the possible futures of our emerging tribes spread out like branches of the World Tree; as varied as the landscapes, plants and creatures that make up this planet with us. With the resurgence of life comes the return of diversity. Whatever is next, I feel that the world we will experience will become many, the tales extraordinary, the reviving beasts and elementals fantastic. Not so much a universe as a multiverse. In honoring the multiverse we afford it the chance to blossom in a range of colors that will not have been witnessed for thousands of years. Perhaps this is a vibrational shift. Perhaps this is simply what life always promised us it could be with our help: magical, profound and loving.

I guess if there's one point to telling this story, it's what it shows us about our power when we believe something to be true. We have the ability to shape life on Earth in the most dramatic ways. We can tell a story, and if it's believed the effects can be enormous. Believing is seeing, as much as seeing is believing. And as we step onwards, aware of our power and responsibility, it's pertinent to remember the way we look at the world. We can find all the examples of how we're going to hell in a handbag. But we can also attend to how we can help. We can be open enough to hear the apocalypse (meaning 'to reveal what was covered'). We can embrace it as the apocalypso and get dancing. We can find even more particular ways that separate us. We can use those distinctions to help us come together in communities. But, ultimately, all we can do is choose the steps we make from here on, accept them as our choices, empower those around us to do likewise, and go forward. And how the world evolves with us will be the stories that years from now, our children's children will hear and share round the fire.

But who knows how these next few years will unfold? I certainly don't. And anyway, I've been banging on for long enough. It's everyone else's turn now.

Acknowledgments

First off, I'd like to thank my loving, wise, compassionate and ever-patient guides for the partnership. My ancestors, especially my dad, Victor, my Nain, Rebecca, and my mum, Nia Wyn, who helped me understand and celebrate the masculine in the female as well as the feminine in the male. And to Margaret Ceridwen and William Jenkins for sheltering me without condition of blood and teaching me how you can tell love by its smell.

More people than I can name have helped me along the path to completing this book. Some directly, by reading draft copies and offering advice, others by helping me keep the faith in myself and my ability to get a book published. A number of writers allowed this book to be written, both by leading the way and lending their words.

Liz and Matthew brought their detailed eye to bear over different sections of the early draft and improved it massively. Jane has been a creative reader and sharer of ideas about the importance of philosophy and the limitations of dogma. Libby has, as ever, been a brilliant, patient and encouraging editor and friend, not to mention the owner of bookshelves that speak volumes.

Simon at the Sacred Trust provided consistent cheerleading and inspirational teaching. Trevor and John at O-books made it possible to even think of writing an acknowledgments chapter, and Mollie's time and patience has made every line of it better.

Imelda has co-created a beautiful picture and has always sung this book's praises, as have all the members of the clan.

Sophie, Rhid, Lou, Lynn, Star, Michael and Erica have given unwavering support and love, and Alex, on top of everything else, dreamt this book would be read before the first word was written (copyright Donna Noble)!

To these friends and many more, to all the green tribe on these islands and beyond, to everyone who believes we could try doing it differently, and to all of you who've got this far …

Thank you.

Bibliography

Chinua Achebe *Things Fall Apart* (1958)
Tariq Ali *The Clash of Fundamentalisms* (2002)
Maya Angelou *The Complete Collected Poems* (1994)
Karen Armstrong *The Battle for God* (2000)
Karen Armstrong *The Great Transformation* (2006)
Karen Armstrong *The History of God* (1993)
Katherine Ashenburg *Clean* (2007)
Bruce Bagemihl *Biological Exuberance* (1999)
Simone de Beauvoir *The Second Sex* (1952)
Alison Benjamin and Brian McCallum *A World Without Bees* (2008)
Bruno Bettelheim *Symbolic Wounds: Puberty Rites and the Envious Male* (1954)
William Bloom (ed.) *The Penguin Book of New Age and Holistic Writing* (2001)
Libby Brooks *The Story of Childhood* (2006)
Dee Brown *Bury My Heart at Wounded Knee* (1970)
Judith Butler *Gender Trouble* (1990)
Simon Buxton *The Shamanic Way of the Bee* (2006)
Beatrix Campbell *Goliath* (1993)
Rachel Carson *Silent Spring* (1963)
Robert Chadwick *First Civilizations* (2005)
Bruce Chatwin *Songlines* (1987)
Stanley Cohen *Folk Devils and Moral Panics* (1972)
Merle Collins *Rotten Pomerack* (1992)
Julian Cope *The Modern Antiquarian* (1998)
Rachel Cusk *A Life's Work* (2008)
Mary Daly *Gyn/Ecology* (1978)
Brian Day *The Modern Pagan* (2006)
J Delaney, J Lipton and E Toth *The Curse: A Cultural History of Menstruation* (1976)
Carol Ann Duffy *Feminine Gospels* (2002)

Carol Ann Duffy *Selected Poems* (1994)
Barbara Ehrenreich *Dancing in the Streets: A History of Collective Joy* (2006)
Barbara Ehrenreich and Deidre English *Witches, Midwives and Nurses: A History of Women Healers* (1973)
Frantz Fanon *Black Skin White Masks* trans. Charles Markmann (1986)
Michael Foreman *Dinosaurs and All That Rubbish* (1974)
Sue Gerhardt *Why Love Matters* (2006)
Al Gore *An Inconvenient Truth* (2006)
Ann Grifalconi *The Village of Round and Square Houses* (1987)
Nicholas Guyatt *Have a Nice Doomsday* (2007)
Graham Hancock *Supernatural* (2005)
Michael Harner *The Way of the Shaman* (1990)
John Heale *One Blood: Inside Britain's Modern Street Gangs* (2008)
Bob Hopkins *The Transition Handbook* (2008)
Erik Hornung *Akhenaten and the Religion of Light* (1999)
Michael Howard *The Sacred Ring: Pagan Origins of British Folk Festivals* (1995)
Jessica Hutchings and Clive Aspin *Sexuality and the Stories of Indigenous People* (2007)
Luce Irigaray *Je, Tu, Nous* (1993)
Luce Irigaray *Key Writings* (2004)
Luce Irigaray *The Language of Men* trans. Erin Carlston (1989)
Henry Jenkins (ed.) *The Children's Culture Reader* (1998)
Matilda Joslyn Gage *Woman, Church and State: The Original Exposé of Male Collaboration against the Female Sex* (1980)
James Kincaid *Child-Loving* (1992)
Eva Knudsen *The Circle and the Spiral: A Study of Australian Aboriginal and New Zealand Maori Literature* (2004)
Bart Kosko *Fuzzy Thinking* (1993)
Kay Dian Kriz *Slavery, Sugar, and the Culture of Refinement* (2008)
Felicity Lawrence *Eat Your Heart Out* (2008)
Gerda Lerner *The Creation of Patriarchy* (1986)

James Lovelock *Gaia: A New Look at Life on Earth* (2000)
James Lovelock *The Revenge of Gaia* (2006)
Richard Mabey *Food for Free* (2004)
Richard Mabey *Nature Cure* (2005)
Sharon McErlane *A Call to Power: The Grandmothers Speak* (2007)
Margaret Mead *Coming of Age in Samoa* (1928)
Margaret Mead *Male and Female* (1950)
George Monbiot *Bring on the Apocalypse* (2008)
Grace Nichols *I is a Long-Memoried Woman* (1983)
Bruce Parry *Tribe* (2007)
Leanne Payne *Crisis in Masculinity* (1988)
F. David Peat *Blackfoot Physics* (1994)
Sadie Plant *Zeros and Ones* (1997)
Roslyn Poignant *Myths and Legends of the South Seas* (1970)
Jill Purce *The Mystic Spiral* (1974)
Gabrielle Roth *Sweat Your Prayers* (1999)
Joan Roughgarden *Evolution's Rainbow: Diversity, Gender and Sexuality in Nature and People* (2004)
Leonard Shlain *The Alphabet versus the Goddess* (2001)
Penelope Shuttle and Peter Redgrove *The Wise Wound* (1978)
Vigdis Songe-Moller *Philosophy without Women* (2002)
Gloria Steinem *Outrageous Acts and Everyday Rebellions* (1984)
Lynn Stephen *Sexualities and Genders in Zapotec Villages* (2002)
Robin Sylvan *Trance Formation: The Spiritual and Religious Dimensions of Global Rave Culture* (2007)
Barbara Tedlock *Woman in the Shaman's Body* (2005)
Alice Walker *Living by the Word* (1988)
Marina Warner *Alone of All Her Sex* (1976)
Jeanette Winterson *The Stone Gods* (2007)
Naomi Wolf *Beauty Myth* (1992)
Virginia Woolf *A Room of One's Own* (1929)
Virginia Woolf *Three Guineas* (1938)